Famine

Methuen Drama

This edition published in 2001 by
Methuen Publishing Limited

Copyright © 1977, 1984, 1992 Tom Murphy

First published in 1977 by The Gallery Press, Dublin, Ireland

Tom Murphy has asserted his rights under the Copyright, Designs
and Patents Act, 1988, to be identified as the author of this work

ISBN 0 413 77123 7

A CIP catalogue record for this book is available at the British Library

Typeset by Wilmaset Ltd, Birkenhead, Wirral
Transferred to digital printing 2005

Famine

by Tom Murphy

Methuen Drama

Famine

To the memory of Jack and Winifred Murphy

Characters

John Connor, *the village leader, aged about 45*
Mother, *his wife, about 40*
Maeve, *his daughter, aged 16*
Donaill, *his son, aged 10*
Dan O'Dea, *a villager, about 65*
Dan's Wife, *about 70*
Liam Dougan, *a villager, mid twenties*
Mark Dineen, *a villager, about 45*
Brian Riordan, *a villager, about 60*
Malachy O'Leary, *a villager, about 25*
Mickeleen O'Leary, *a villager, about 30*
Father Horan, *a curate, about 35*
First Policeman, *about 50*
Second Policeman, *about 30*
Clancy, *a merchant, about 50*
Captain Shine, *a landlord, about 50*
Mr Simmington, *an agent for an absentee landlord, about 40*
Father Daly, *Parish Priest, about 65*
Justice of the Peace, *about 65*
Other Villagers

Time and place:
Autumn 1846 to Spring 1847 in rural Ireland.

Scene One

The Wake

A Sunday afternoon, Autumn, 1846, in the village of Glanconor.

Brian *is sitting on a ditch by the roadside outside John Connor's house.* **Mark** *is coming from John Connor's house to join* **Brian**. *Behind the ditch is the potato crop.*

Dan *and his* **Wife** *enter on the road and go to John Connor's house. They pause in the doorway.*

Dan   The Lord have mercy on the soul of the dead!

People in the House   The Lord have mercy on us all!

In the house, John Connor's daughter is being waked. **Dan** *shakes hands with the chief mourners:* **John**, **Mother** (**John**'s **Wife**), **Maeve** *and* **Donaill**; *then he kneels by the corpse and prays.* **Dan**'s **Wife** *sits with* **Mother**.

As the following develops into a keen, **John** *leaves the house and stands outside the door. He is followed by* **Donaill**.

Dan's Wife   Cold and silent is now her bed.

Others   Yes.

Dan's Wife   Damp is the blessed dew of night,
But the sun will bring warmth and heat in the
morning and dry up the dew.

Others   Yes.

Mother   But her heart will feel no heat from the sun.

Others   No!

Dan's Wife   Nor no more the track of her feet in the dew.

Others   No!

Dan's Wife   Nor the sound of her step in the village of
Connor,
Where she was ever foremost among young
women.

Others   No!

Dan's Wife   Cold and silent is now her bed.

Others   Yes.

Liam *enters. He shakes hands with* **John**. *He stands in the doorway.*

Liam   The Lord have mercy on the soul of the dead!

People in the House   The Lord have mercy on us all!

Liam *shakes hands with the chief mourners, kneels by the corpse and prays.*

Mother   My sunshine, she was!

Others   Yes.

Mother   I loved her better nor the sun itself!

Others   Yes.

Mother   And when I see the sun go down
I think of my girl and my black night of sorrow.
But a dark storm came on
And my sunshine was lost to me forever;
My girl cannot return.

Others   No!

Mother   Cold and silent is now her bed.

Others   Yes.

*Dan leaves the house and stands with **John** outside the door, respectfully silent for a few moments. **John** is staring vacantly at the crop of potatoes.*

Dan   . . . A quare softness in it, Johnny? . . . A bad Summer? . . . It was, a mac. Dry and drought and then the rain . . . But we saved the oats?

John (*to himself*)   How am I to overcome it?

Dan   Hah? . . . Oh now, she's in a better place: May she rest in peace . . . What do you think of the piaties? (*Potatoes.*)

John (*to himself*)   Oh, what does it matter!

*He turns abruptly and goes into the house followed by **Donaill**.*

*Dan joins **Mark** and **Brian** who are sitting on the ditch.*

Dan   How the men!

Mark } Hah-hah, Danny!
Brian } Dan!

Dan   Poor Johnny is upset. And he should be getting used to it now.

Brian   Oh, yis.

A silence.

Mark (*nervous staccato voice*)   But – but – but, ye see, last year the first crop failed but the main crop was good, and this year the first crop failed, but the main crop will be – will be – will be . . .

Dan   Hah?

Brian   Oh, you could be right.

Liam comes out of the house and joins them. A silence.

Mark   But – but – but, we didn't see none of that quare fog we had last year?

Liam   What?

Brian   No.

Mark   Isn't that what I'm saying? And that crop in there
now – (*He points to the crop but then quickly changes his mind.*)
That's what you'd call the ghostly fog. Last year. The
clouds of it rolling –

Liam } That wasn't why –
Mark } Not wanting to rise, but clinging to the stalks, and
　　　　　 slow. And sure what piatie could grow right with
　　　　　 it . . . We had nothing like that this year?

Liam   We had the rain, we had the –

Brian } No faith now, we had narys the fog.
Dan } That's correct, Marcus.

Mark   Certainly! And – and – and I seen my own crop
last year, and the stalks as black as – as – as – as . . .

Dan   And 'twas the fog caused that.

Brian   Oh, yis.

Liam   Ach!

Mark   Yis! And what's on them in there now today but a
few speckeleens the flies'd cause?

Brian   Oh, you could be right.

Dan   But tell me this, and tell me no more . . . (*Joking;
lowering his voice, mysteriously.*) what caused the fog?

Mark   Cause 'twas a terrible year last year.

Liam (*winks at* **Brian**, *then*)   What, tell us, Danny?

Dan (*finger to his lips*)   Oh, the less said about that party
the better.

They laugh.

Mark (*forcing a laugh*)   The – the – the less said about the
sidheog (*Or 'the fairies'.*) the better.

Dan   Ye won't heed me: Well, here's someone that ye'll heed (let ye ask his opinion).

Brian (*looks off at someone approaching; then*)   Oh, we'll be right enough.

Fr Horan *enters.*

Fr Horan   Bail o Dhia oraibh! (*God bless you!*)

Men   Go mba shé dhuit. (*The same blessing on you.*)

Fr Horan   Our prayers for fine weather are answered, I'm thinking.

Mark   They are, they are, Father.

Liam   If it isn't too late.

Fr Horan   Wha'? (*Looks at crop, but only for a moment.*) Trust in God.

Dan   There was nothing on them this morning getting up, d'ye know.

Fr Horan   Wha'?

Mark   Speckles.

Liam   Do you think –

Fr Horan   Sure I'm not a farmer, Dougan.

Mark   Last – last – last year was the bad year.

Fr Horan   God is good.

Dan   And he has a good mother.

Brian   He has.

Fr Horan   He has, he has indeed.

Liam   But would you say it'd be alright if we dug a few of them to see if –

Fr Horan   I saw you late into mass again this morning, Brian.

Brian　Oh –

Fr Horan (*mimicking him*)　Oh! Oh!

Brian　Aaa, I'm a slow sleeper, Father.

They laugh.

Fr Horan (*leaving them*)　Be good, men!

Fr Horan *goes into the house. A silence.*

Mark　Well, I – I – I heard of a priest one time that was a blister from the pulpit: They say he was one Sunday charging his flock about the drinking and the poteen. ''Tis the drinking,' says he, 'as makes ye go home and beat your wives and your childre, and neglect your crops and your duties, and shoot at the landlord,' says he, 'and miss'. And miss. (*They laugh*).

Brian　Oh now, that's only a yarn.

Mark　And miss!

Dan　He wasn't a home-produced priest anyway if he mentioned the shooting. Moral force, boys. They learn a different class of Latin now entirely.

Liam　Moral force.

Dan (*importantly*)　The polocy. (*Policy.*)

Liam　Daniel O'Connell's crowd in Dublin.

Dan　And the clergy all over.

Brian　Oh, we'll be alright.

Dan　And I heard 'tis the Queen herself, and not the Pope, is writing the books for all now.

Liam (*winks at* **Brian**)　Correct. And doesn't she send a pound to O'Connell every week of the year!

Dan　To 'The Liberator' is it?

Brian　And a kiss every time she meets him.

Dan   Hah? (**Brian** *chuckles*.) Ara, hanam mo ndiabhail! May the divil sweep ye! (*They laugh*.)

Brian (*chuckling*)   Victoria!

Liam (*chuckling*)   Victoria!

Dan (*chuckling*)   Vic-tore-eeaaaa!

Mark   Give over, will ye. Is it any wonder −

Dan (*laughing*)   Oh, you can always, Marcus, put a bag on your back, like many another done, and take to the roads if they fail.

Brian   Aw, whist, Danny.

Silence.

Liam   But if we knew − Hah? If there was something we could − Hah? If there was someone to −

Dan   Someone to −

Liam   Tell us what to . . .

Dan   Yis.

Instinctively, they look towards the house. **John** *comes out of house and stands outside the door, head bowed.* **Donaill** *follows him, stands beside him, tugs at* **John**'*s coat.*

Brian   And that's the second one he's lost.

Dan   But he'll think of something brave for us yet.

Brian   Oh, sure he will.

Mark   If − if − if it's needed.

Dan   If it's needed, boys. The Connors would do the brave thing always.

John *is conscious of the men watching him.* **Donaill** *tugs at* **John**'*s coat again.* **John** *turns on the boy, his fist raised as if to squash the boy into the ground.*

John (*angrily*)   You're under my feet!

He pauses, his fist raised, seeing the boy's surprise and hurt. Gently.

Don't be under my feet, a mac.

He goes to the gable end of the house, trying to suppress his grief and perplexity.

Fr Horan *comes out of house. He looks sympathetically after* **John**. *He takes* **Donaill**'s *hand and leads him off, taking him for a walk.*

Fr Horan   Is there but one true church?

Donaill   Although there may be many sects, there is but one true church.

Fr Horan   Good man. And how do you call the true church?

Donaill   The Roman Catholic Church.

Fr Horan   And why are we obliged to be of that true church?

Donaill   Because none can be saved out of it.

Fr Horan   Good man. And who are those who do not believe what God has taught?

Donaill   Heretics and infidels.

Fr Horan   Good. And . . .

Fr Horan *and* **Donaill** *have gone. Through the following,* **John** *goes into the house.*

Brian   Oh, he's bright enough with it.

Dan   Well, I remember in '17 – and the comical-est thing – I seen the youngsters and the hair falling out of their heads and then starting growing on their faces.

Brian   And in '36 –

Liam   I seen the likes. I seen –

Dan }   You did not!
Liam }   I did! – I seen –

Brian⎫ The worse I seen –
Dan ⎭ You did not! And in '22 –

Liam⎫ I seen – I seen –
Dan ⎭ You didn't! And in '22 – in '22 –

Brian⎫ The worse I seen –
Liam⎭ Well, I seen '36, didn't I? And '40, and '41!

Brian⎫ The worse I seen was a child –
Dan ⎭ In '22 – In '22 – In '22! I counted eleven dead by
the roadside and my own father one of them. Near
the water, Clogher bridge, and the rats. I'm
afeared of them since.

Brian   A child, an infant –

Dan   And some I seen, green from eating the grass, and
yellow and black from fever and the divil-knows-what.

Brian   A child under a bush, eating its mother's breast.
And she dead and near naked.

Mark   But only speckles.

Liam   And last year, '45.

Dan   Sure, you weren't here at all last year.

Liam   Well, didn't my mother go last year?

Mark   She was old –

Liam   Starved!

Mark   Old –

Liam   Starved! To keep what few piaties we had for seed
for that crop in there. Isn't it the same way John Connor
starved that daughter of his that went last night. Wasn't
that his plan? The meeting he called: to keep what little
piaties we had for seed.

Brian   Oh, you're alright, Liam.

Liam   And now a wake – Like we done! Flaithuil
(*Generous.*) with food, drink and tobaccy. And cannot
afford it in life or death! And what kind of plan is that?

Brian   We'll be alright.

Dan   Well, Daniel O'Connell –

Brian   We'll be alright.

Dan   Sure, he's a great man, the finest, 'The Liberator',
sure, isn't he?

Mark   But only speckeleens.

Dan   Only speckles, Mark.

Brian   We'll be alright.

Evening is coming on and it is growing dark. **Malachy** *enters,*
glancing behind him a few times. He joins the men at the ditch.

Dan   Good man, Malachy!

Brian   Malachy, a mac!

Silence.

Mark   Hah? . . . But, sure – sure – sure, there's no sense
at all in what ye're saying. How do ye know what's under
them yet? They're not black. And there's no change in
them in the last few hours. Ye see, last year the first crop
failed but the main crop was good, but this year the first
crop failed but the main crop – that crop in there – will be
– (*To* **Liam** *who starts to move.*) Stand your ground,
Dougan, and don't go bringing any class of bad luck by
rooting on a Sunday!

Liam (*annoyed*)   Ach, I wasn't going near them! (*He sees*
Mickeleen *approaching.*) Here's your brother coming,
Malachy.

Malachy (*to himself*)   Chris-jays, if he keeps following me!

Malachy *leaves as the hunchbacked figure of* **Mickeleen** *arrives.*

Mickeleen (*shouting after* **Malachy**)   Pay your respects!
Pay your respects! I'm not following you at all! Run! Run
then! Off to England again! (*He glares at the group beside the
ditch.*) What are the big men watching? (*Then he laughs at
them.*) Why don't ye root a few and see? Can ye not see the
foretelling spotted leaf? The sourness is still in the clay.
Smell it! Smell it! Ye don't want to see, but in a day or
three, the smell will blind ye into seeing!

He laughs, goes to the house and stands in the doorway.

The Lord have mercy on the soul of the dead!

People in the House (*after a slight pause*)   The Lord have
mercy on us all!

Mickeleen (*standing over corpse*)   She was lovely.

People in the House   She was.

Mickeleen   She was civil.

People in the House   She was.

Mickeleen   Even to the cripple . . . not like some. She
was regal. And why wouldn't she? A descendent of the
Connors, kings and chieftains here in days of yore. A true
Connor, she was, of this village, Glanconor, called after the
Connors. She's an angel now. She was an angel on earth.
And we won't forget her. Or forget it for *them*. And blessed
will be the day or the night when instruments will scald the
rotten hearts of them responsible. And blessed will be the
earth, cause 'twill refuse them graves, but spew up their
packages for the fox and the dog, the rat and the bird.

Mother (*looks to* **John** *to reply*)   . . . We know nothing of
that kind of talk here.

Mickeleen   You're a king, Seán Connor, and I'm sorry
for your trouble, as ye were sorry for mine, when my
mother and my father – that put this (*Hump.*) on me with
his stick – rotted on the hillside. And my brother of the
great stature was off roving, having his spate of pleasuring
in England. And ye here, kings and all, afeared of the

bodack landlord and his bodack agent to give the cripple and his mother and father shelter.

Mother   I'm asking you, Michael O'Leary, not to go bringing disgrace on the dead child's bed. (*She looks to* **John** *again to reply.*) Welcome be the holy will of God.

John   Let him talk. 'Tis his right to talk. He means no harm.

Mickeleen   Phy (*Why.*) would I mean harm, Seán. I'm sorry for your troubles and for all your troubles to come. (*He sits abruptly*).

Mother (*looking at* **John**)   We're thankful.

John   We're thankful to ye all.

Mickeleen (*taunting*)   Hah, Seán?

John   Drink. Drink up. Pass round the pipes, Sinéad. Bring out more food, Maeve. Call the fiddler. 'Tis a poor class of a wake ye're giving *my* daughter.

Mickeleen   But how will you overcome it, Seán? Or are you another pleb refusing to smell the sourness again?

John (*he goes to the corpse*)   We can't send them off mean . . . She *was* regal . . . And – we – won't – send – them off mean, in spite of – in spite of – whatever! Welcome be the holy will of God. No matter what He sends 'tis our duty to submit. And blessed be His name, even for this, and for anything else that's to come. He'll grace us to withstand it.

Mickeleen *laughs as* **John** *goes outside.*

Preparations begin for the festive part of the wake. Talk grows louder, people laugh, smoke, eat and drink. Off, behind house, the **Fiddler** *is playing a tune and the dancing has begun.*

Outside it is dark. The men at the ditch are reluctant to leave their vigil. **John** *watches them.*

Dan   The sport is starting up. Will we be going over?

Silence.

Mark   But – but – but, and that government official that came by in June. The writing down he did, the Lord save us!

Liam   A hundred of the same government officials came by and went, writing down, and things is only getting worse, and what do you reckon that means?

Mark   What – what – what do you reckon, Dougan?

Liam   Ach!

John (*calls*)   Are ye not coming over?

Mark   Ach! Ach, phat? (*What?*) Ach, phat, Dougan? Ye weren't the only ones had death in your house through the year – Ach, phat! – And – and – and your rent wasn't ruz in the middle of it.

Liam   Well, maybe we weren't trying to do 'swanky' on it, white-washing the outside of our house.

Mark   And isn't that my business?

John } Are ye coming over?
Liam } 'Tis, 'tis, 'tis, that's your business, ach phat!

At this stage the mourners are coming out of the house, listening to the row.

Mark   Some people like the dirty word always!

Liam   And they like splitting paupers' skulls wide open too!

John } Is this what ye come here for?
Mark } Some people – some people like the dirty word. And the dirty deed. And it's men like some here, doubtin' – doubtin' – doubtin', no heed or faith to Him that's above, or what He can do, will make Him change His mind. And I seen men like some here heel cartloads of the finest of lumpers into hollows in the fields one time, and there's some of us was ever careful and never wasted, and we're suffering for their likes.

Liam   Stand away from me, Danny, I'll not touch the pauper.

Brian⎫   You're alright, Marcus.
Mark⎭   Pauper yourself, Dougan! Pauper yourself! With
the dirty mouth! And where's the man with – the
– dirty – word's proof? Are they black are they?
Are they black? Are they? Are they? Are they
black? Are they black?

John   Is this yere respect for a dead Connor?

John *pushes them aside roughly and jumps over the ditch into the field. He roots some plants, scattering them about him, digging in the earth with his hands. Then he holds out his hands to them, showing them the blighted potatoes.*

(*Quietly.*) Ach phat now?

Pause. They stare, dumbfounded, at his hands for a few moments, then at the field. **Mark** *takes the bad potatoes from* **John**.

Liam   What are we going to do?

Dan   . . . Hah?

Mark   We should have et (*Eaten.*) the seed.

Liam   Maybe we should have sowed them deeper.

Brian   Maybe if we leave them for a while . . .

Dan   . . . Hah?

Mark   The fog if we expose them.

Liam   John?

Dan   The sunshine might dry them – or – But it might
damage them too if . . .

Mark   We should have et the seed.

Dan   Johnny?

John   Dig them, first light, and maybe save some of
them. Then we'll see.

Mickeleen *has pushed his way through the mourners. He starts to laugh.*

Mickeleen   Did ye think '46 wouldn't folly (*Follow.*) '45? That bad doesn't folly bad? That all is to be bad! That ye'll all folly my style of thinking yet!

Mark   Aa, get – get – get up off your knees, you gadhahaun!

And at the same time he throws the rotten potatoes at **Mickeleen***.*

Suddenly **Mark***'s remark and action seem funny; excepting* **John***, the crowd, laughing and shouting, start to chase* **Mickeleen** *off. The chase turns into a dance. The wake is in full-swing. The whole is a scene of revelry.*

It grows lighter and the noise gradually subsides as morning comes on. The lid is put on the coffin, and as it is being carried off, followed by mourners, **Mother** *keens.*

Mother   Life blood of my heart –
For the sake of my girl I cared only for this world.
She was brave, she was generous,
she was loved by rich and poor.
She was comely, she was clear-skinned.
And when she laughed – Did ye hear?
And her hair – Did ye see? –
Golden like the corn.
But why should I tell what everyone knows?
Why go back to what never can be more?
She who was everything to me is dead.
She is gone forever.
She will return no more.
No!
Cold and silent is her repose.

Mother *exits following the others.*

Scene Two

The Moral Force

Off, the noise of a convoy of corn-carts on a road. The noise continues throughout the scene.

The scene is the same as before. It is a few weeks later.

Mark, **Brian** and **Mickeleen** *are standing or sitting on the ditch, watching the convoy, counting the carts.*

Contrasting with them, **John** *and* **Maeve** *are working in the field behind the ditch:* **John** *is redigging;* **Maeve** *is foraging with her hands.*

Brian   That's fifteen.

Mark (*calling to* **John**)   The fifteenth one passing!

John *and* **Maeve** *do not look up.* **Mickeleen** *laughs.*

Mickeleen   Hah, Seán?

Brian   The sixteenth coming.

Mark   Sixteenth, coming!

Mickeleen (*calling*)   Hah, Maeveen? Would you like a maum (*A handful.*) of oats out of one of them carts?

Maeve   Would *you* get it for me?

Mickeleen (*laughs*)   Oh, that's for the ports. To the ports of soft English bellies. Not that I'm saying yours isn't . . . soft.

John (*calls*)   Look about you, girl. Them nettles yonder.

Mickeleen   Hah, Seán? 'Twas another mistake to dig them too soon?

Mark   The seventeenth!

Brian   The eightcenth coming.

Mickeleen (*calling*)   Don't stoop too low, Maeveen! (*She mutters something, not looking up.*) . . . Hah? . . . Where was your hand this morning when you woke up, Maeveen?

Maeve (*childish outburst*)   Mickeleen Cam! (*Twisted.*) Mickeleen Cam! Mickeleen Cam!

John (*approaching*)   Bi 'do thost, girl! (*Hold your tongue, girl.*) Is that a críochán (*Potato.*) over there?

Maeve   A stone, a stone! You got everything good that was in it the last time you dug it.

John   I got a few middling ones: Take them in.

Maeve *takes the potatoes and gives them to* **Mother** *who is in the house.*

Brian   The nineteenth.

Mark   But why are they exporting it so early this year?

Mickeleen   Hah, Seán?

John (*quietly*)   Because I think they're afeared we'll eat it.

Mark   Begobs no fear of us doing . . . (*He breaks off, laughing nervously.*)

Dan *and* **Liam** *arrive, an excitement about them: they are followed by* **Dan**'s **Wife** *who arrives a few seconds later.*

Dan   There's a cart −

Liam   Pulling this way −

Dan   To join the convoy ablow (*Below.*) −

Liam   And Malachy and others trailing behind it!

Brian   And the soldiers, no doubt, 'round it?

Liam   No! −

Dan   Only a couple of the police, just, and the driver. Hah?

Liam   There's enough of us in it.

Dan   Hah? Johnny?

Mickeleen   Get the stones, get the stones!

Mark   Yis!

Mickeleen   We'll leather the vastard peelers. (*Police.*)

John   One cart won't do much for us.

Mark   We have a rights to live!

John   Not of other people's property.

Liam (*incredulous*)   . . . What?

Dan   What's upsetting you, Johnny?

John   Where would the world be if any could come and take what he felt like?

Liam   . . . What!

Mickeleen   Stone the rotten bodacks!

Liam   But what are we going to do?

John   What's right!

The statement seems to surprise himself as much as it does the others.

. . . What's right. And maybe, that way, we'll make no mistakes.

Liam   But –

John   We done the likes before and where did it get us?

Mark   But the bad year it's going to be.

Mickeleen (*laughs*)   'Twill be the worst ever!

John   They're always right: We'll be right too.

Liam   But how are we to live?

John   Go home: Redig: We dug them fields too fast and, I'm sure, missed a lot that's edible. And collect up whatever roots and nettles ye can.

Mickeleen   Roots and weeds are for the pigs! –

John   And not be using up whatever cabbage and turnips ye have left –

Mickeleen   Get sticks, stones –

John   I got a few críocháns in there today –

Mickeleen   Look! It's coming –

John   I'm calling a meeting tonight and a fair say for everyone! Then we'll see.

Mickeleen   Look! It's coming! We'll stone them now while we're able.

John   It's easy for you! All you want is to cause trouble. You have nothing to lose.

Mickeleen (*holding his crotch*)   I've still my budgeen as good as another!

John   Stand in off the road. I ask you gently.

Mark (*taking a kick at* **Mickeleen**)   Stand in, you – you – you – you –

John (*restraining* **Mark**)   'Asy. 'Asy. (*To himself, as if to convince himself.*) It's not the way . . . 'Asy now.

The cart is heard approaching.

First Policeman *enters, clearing stones off the road. Followed a few seconds later by* **Second Policeman**. *As scene progresses a crowd gathers, including* **Malachy**, **Mother** *and* **Maeve**.

First Policeman (*wary*)   Good day to ye!

Mickeleen *picks up a stone and throws it aside, as if helping the* **Policeman**.

(*To* **Mickeleen**) Stand in, a mac, there's a wagon passing in a minute.

Mickeleen   We won't eat it.

First Policeman   Hah?

John   Stand in, Michael.

Second Policeman   What is it?

First Policeman   Clear the way like a good boy.

Mickeleen   We won't eat it!

Second Policeman   Move! Out of the way! Move in! (*He pushes* **Mickeleen** *back*.)

John   'Asy, and he will.

Mickeleen (*sees* **Malachy** *is close by*)   Ara what? Ara what? Do ye think you're big gallant soldiers or what? (*The* **Policeman** *hesitates*.) . . . They're afeared of us!

Mark   They're afeared we'll eat it! Yahoo!

Second Policeman   Close up now, or I'll soon fasten your tongue.

Malachy (*stepping in*)   Never attempt that, peeler.

Liam   We're hungry! –

Dan   Hit him, Malachy! –

Mark   We're hungry – we're hungry – we're hungry! –

Liam   Why should we starve? – And look at it!

The cart has stopped, off.

John   'Asy.

First Policeman   We've orders for no trouble now.

Second Policeman   But we'll take trouble.

John   'Asy, let ye.

Liam   Do ye want to starve us?

First Policeman   Back! Sure the real hunger didn't start at all yet.

Mark   We grew that oats.

Second Policeman   And sold it – back! Back or I'll – If ye wanted to eat it ye should have done, and not sold it.

John (*losing control for a moment*)   And what'd pay the rent for us then?

First Policeman   That's it, ye can't have it two sides!

Mickeleen   Take it, and leather them! What are ye waiting for?

John   Stop, will ye!

First Policeman   Think of yere homes let some of ye –

Mickeleen   The cart! Break it! Smash it!

Second Policeman *goes for* **Mickeleen**, **Malachy** *moves to intercept him.* **John** *throws* **Malachy** *back, pushes* **Second Policeman** *aside, and grabs* **Mickeleen**.

John (*to* **Policeman**)   Take yere cart the other way. There's no one here that'll hinder ye!

The Police are leaving, we hear the corn cart moving off, and peace is being restored as **Fr Horan** *arrives. He is too hot and bothered to see that the trouble is over.*

Fr Horan   What's going on here? Out of the way! Ye were going to show yourselves as wild savages, were ye?

John   It's all over now, Father.

Fr Horan   What's the stick for, Dineen? Put it down at once! I command you!

John   It's all over now.

Fr Horan   Stand back, Connor! Is it that ye wanted to go breaking the laws of God and man? Didn't I see ye and I coming down from the hill above.

Liam   We're hungry.

Fr Horan   Stand where you are, Dougan!

Mickeleen   The bodacks of vastards don't want us to live!

Fr Horan   Oh-ho, O'Leary, didn't I know you'd be in it!

Liam   They're sweeping the country bare –

Mickeleen   And are ye going heeding another that bids
ye starve?

Fr Horan   Come down off the ditch, O'Leary.

Mark   We're going to starve?

Mickeleen   Yis, that's what they want to do to us!

Fr Horan   Come down off the ditch –

Mickeleen ⎱   They want to starve us! And look at it!
Christ, the wagon-loads of it!

Fr Horan ⎰   A curse on the first man to move! Are my
eyes deceiving me? Do ye realise the great
God is above in heaven watching ye? And
His blessed Mother this minute shedding
down tears of sorrow. Merciful Jesus forgive
us!·

John   It's all over now.

Mickeleen   Christ, ye're letting it go!

Fr Horan   And if it be Thy Holy will, straighten that
wretch on the ditch. Give us back our forbearance, our
patience – Our saintliness, O'Leary! The fine character of
this village –

Mickeleen   There'll be no village –

Fr Horan   Stop!

Mickeleen   Why should I stop? –

Fr Horan   Stop! –

Mark   Stop, O'Leary! –

Fr Horan   Do you believe in God at all, O'Leary? The
one true God, or in His church, or His ministers, or in His
goodness? And especially His goodness to you and
tolerance: that He doesn't strike you down dead this
minute! No wonder the hump is on you!

John   It's all over now.

Fr Horan   I saw the devil here today. Weren't ye warned that it's in hard times he strikes most? Can ye forget the great God so easy? He knows about our grievances and He's taking account of them and He won't forget them! And won't we win in the long run?

John } 'Asy, your reverence.
Fr Horan } Aren't we on the right path? The pride we had that we could say we had no physical force men in this parish. And we got our religious freedom that way, in '29, O'Connell's way, without a blow struck – Stay where you are, O'Leary! But that a proved heretic can stand up here and start the devil's work: Anarchy, fight, the pike, the gun! – Where would it end? – Strike! – Maul! – Maim! – Wreck! – And destroy! – Tear limb from limb! – Butchery! – Murder! – Blood and destruction! – Let it flow on this holy ground – Yis, Murder! – And ye were ready to murder – Butchery and gore! What advantage is worth a single drop of blood?

Mickeleen   Jesus shed his blood!

Fr Horan   To think that he did, and for you!

Malachy (*sensing new danger; quietly to* **Mickeleen**)   Stop!

Fr Horan   Come down off the ditch, O'Leary!

Mickeleen   The men of '98 shed their blood!

Fr Horan   Haven't we had enough trouble with you?

Mickeleen   Were they murderers?

Mark   They were! They were! They were!

Malachy (*to* **Mickeleen**)   Stop, pleb.

Mickeleen   And the priests – the real priests – who led and fought and died – were they murderers?

Fr Horan   Oh, the twist is in your mind along with your body.

Mickeleen   Answer that one!

Fr Horan   I thought the drop in you was black, but did I think –

Mickeleen   And when the tithe war was fought again' the Protestants –

Malachy }   Stop pleb.
Mark   }   Get him down!

Mickeleen   There was little talk from ye about spilling blood!

Fr Horan   O'Leary, don't talk you about Protestants! Didn't you take the soup from them last year? Didn't you?

John   'Asy, 'asy –

Mickeleen   I did! I did! But I didn't say the words for them.

Fr Horan   And damned your eternal soul! –

Malachy   Others here took it! –

Mickeleen   Because I pretended I couldn't talk English –

Fr Horan   You took the bowl of infidel soup –

Mickeleen   And when they gave me their book to kiss –

Fr Horan   And entered into league straightaway with the devil –

Mickeleen   I held it like this –

Fr Horan   And I say here and now –

Mickeleen   But 'twas my *thumb* I kissed! My thumb!

Fr Horan (*roars*)   And – I – say – here – and – now, that the religion that has to depend on starvation to swell its puny misguided flock is double damned!

The crowd is angry, pressing forward towards **Mickeleen**.

Maeve ⎫ Souper! Souper!
Malachy ⎭ Others here took it.
Dan ⎫ Did I take it? Did I take it?
John ⎭ Stand back will ye!
Mark ⎫ Welt him! Welt him!
Mother ⎭ Knock him!
John ⎫ Stand back!
Maeve ⎭ Kick him!
John ⎫ (*pushing* **Maeve** *out of the crowd and shaking her*).
⎭ What's coming over you?

Fr Horan   Keep back there!

Mickeleen (*above the hub-bub*)   And I'd take it the same way again to stay alive!

Fr Horan   Keep back, I say! Keep – You would! You would!

Suddenly, he lashes **Mickeleen** *on the legs with his stick,* **Mickeleen** *falls to the ground. The crowd close in, arms and legs working.*

Mark ⎫ Welt him!
Mother ⎭ Kick him! Kick him!
Maeve ⎫ Flake him! Flake him!
Mark ⎭ Kill him! Kill him!
Malachy ⎫ Leigh amach é! Leigh amach é! (*Let*
⎭ *him out! Let him out!*)

Fr Horan *has the stick raised again to hit* **Mickeleen**. **John** *wrenches it from him.* **Malachy** *and* **John** *fighting off the crowd.* **Fr Horan** *being tossed about in the middle of it.*

Fr Horan   I n-aimm Dé! (*In God's name!*) . . . What's come over ye? . . . Stop!

John   Let out the O'Learys! . . . Clear back! . . . Give over! . . . Have sense! (*Swinging the stick.*) Will ye stop now, will ye!

Eventually they stop, mainly through **John**'s *swinging the stick about him in a circle to clear them back.* **Mickeleen** *is unconscious on the ground.*

Fr Horan (*near tears*)   Get him home will you, Malachy, for the love of God.

Malachy (*savagely, inarticulate*)   'Hat – phat – home – 'hat – phare?!

John   Take him into the house. (*To* **Liam**.) Help him.

Malachy *and* **Liam** *drag* **Mickeleen** *into* **John**'s *house.*

Now, go home the rest of ye.

Dan   You'll think of something for us, Johnny?

John   Go home! Have sense! Go on now! (*They start to move off.*)

Fr Horan (*on the point of tears*)   Off . . . ye vagabones . . . or I'll have ye up before . . . the parish priest. (*He turns away to hide his tears.*) . . . And if there's any more of this kind of . . .

John   . . . Go on now!

John, **Maeve** *and* **Fr Horan** *remain.* **John** *returns the stick to* **Fr Horan**.

Ara, they didn't mean it. They don't mean to be this way. It's only the hunger.

Fr Horan   Hold your tongue, Connor. Be off with you.

John (*to* **Maeve**)   Get inside!

He pushes her in front of him into the house.

Fr Horan *leans against the ditch, crying. The last sounds of the convoy of corn-carts fade in the distance.*

Scene Three

The Resolution

The scene is the same as before. Night.

John *stands outside his house looking out into the night.*

Mother *comes out of house for a basket of turf. (In the house, are* **Maeve**, **Donaill**, **Dan**, **Brian**, **Liam**, **Malachy** *and* **Mickeleen**.)

Silence.

John   I don't think any of the others will come. I thought Marcus might, or . . .

Mother   Are they going to be there stuck in the hearth all night?

John   We'll talk for a while and see what to do.

Mother   I want to feed the childre. Or do you see them anymore: the eyes getting bigger in their heads?

John   Hah? . . . Surely we can share the weeds?

Mother   There's a can of the cow's blood in it too. And I doubt the same poor creature of a beast will stand up to much more bleeding.

John (*to himself*)   I don't know what to tell them. (*He is about to go in.*)

Mother   Johnny.

John   And the devil is ready to rule the world if we allow him.

Mother   What's meetings to do with us?

John   And that will be worse for us as always.

Mother   Neglecting your own. What class of change is coming over you?

John   Hah?

Mother   You're going astray on us.

John   Hah?

Mother   We've lost enough of them.

John   'Hat? I'll look after them!

Mother   Will you? . . . There's no one inside there has anything to do with you but your own. Yis! That seafóideen (*Senile.*) O'Dea is wily. And, believe you me, them Dougans is foxy too, with more stores laid in at home than we'll ever hear of. Them all sparing their turf, while we put on the roaring fires for them.

John   Ara, whist –

Mother   Yis! And them auld O'Learys, having them there, squinting with venom across the floor at each other. That's the country we have. They'll all live on their bitterness and devilry, and where will you be?

John   I'll be – I'll be – And I've found my way to live too!

Mother   And where will *we* be then?

John   What are you saying woman? . . . You're mistaking me. I'll do nothing wrong anymore. It's only by right that we can hope at all now.

Mother   What's right? What's right in a country when the land goes sour? Where is a woman with childre when nature lets her down?

John   Oh, whist woman, you don't know what you're saying.

Mother (*bitterly*)   No.

John   Is there a mark or a blemish on any of ours inside there?

Mother   We've lost two of them!

John   Is any of them like the childre your father reared or my father?

Mother   We've lost –

John   These times is to be different. Believe that! You must! There's lots can be done.

Mother   These times is for *anything* that puts a bit in your own mouth.

John   'Hat? . . . What are you saying?

Mother   Hoarding their fine stacks of turf.

John   'Hat?

Mother   In their yards: their turf: flour can be got for turf in the town.

John (*he gets the insinuation*)   . . . What would you have me do?

Mother   Nothing!

John   Then hould your whist! You're the one that's going astray, I think.

Mother (*this time a plead to him*)   I'm only asking then: don't get lost on us, in meetings or what's right, and forget us.

John   But you're mistaking me. I'll do nothing wrong. (*She turns away from him.*) – I'm doing what I can. And if a time comes when something better is to be done, for you or childre, I'll do it. Be sure of that. And them inside has always come to this house. It's expected of me.

Mother *starts to fill her basket with turf.* **John** *goes into the house.*

In the house, the elation of the corn-cart incident is still with them **Dan** *is cavorting about, mimicking* **Fr Horan**. **Maeve**, **Donaill**, **Liam** *and* **Brian** *enjoy his performance.* **Malachy**, *dour and morose, mutters occasionally to himself, glancing at*

Mickeleen, *who lies on a bed of straw at his feet.* **Mickeleen** *is fully conscious. There is a pot on the fire.*

Dan } 'The Mother of God shedding down tears of sorrow!
. . . Murder! The pike! The gun!'

Brian } (*chuckling*)   Yis . . . Sure yis . . . Yis.
Dan } 'I n-aimm Dé!'

Liam } 'What's come over ye!'
Dan } 'I command ye!'

Liam } But the peelers were frightened.
Brian } Oh, they were, sure.

Dan } 'Do ye realise the great God is watching ye?'
John } Ye were lucky he didn't excommunicate the lot of ye.

Dan } 'Stand back, Connor!'
Liam } 'Stand back, Connor, when you're told!'

They laugh.

Mother *enters with turf.*

They become silent.

Brian   Musha, the creature was only trying to do his job.

Malachy (*to himself*)   Ary yis-yis-yis-yis-yis-yis.

Silence.

John   Well, I don't think anyone else is coming.

Dan   You thought of something for us, Johnny?

John   Well . . . The thing now is . . . I'm sure there's lots we can do, if we all think.

Silence.

Well, I was saying about redigging and collecting up –

Liam   Sure the most of us has done that.

John   Well, for them that hasn't. Everyone to be doing something more than waiting until . . . until . . .

Dan   Until what, Johnny?

He does not know.

Liam   A plan, isn't it, we need?

John   No. Yis. And some class of relief committee is meeting in the town to see about their plan.

Dan (*defiantly*)   But they can't stop us making a plan.

Brian   Oh, they can not.

John   No, what I'm saying is –

Liam   Something useful to be doing, John.

John   Yes.

Silence.

Dan   Repeal!

Liam   Ary, that's only alright for persons in the town to be interested in.

Silence.

Brian   We'll get nothing off the merchants.

Dan (*chuckles*)   We will not, Brian. Off Clancy or the others. We know that.

Brian (*chuckles*)   We do.

Dan   We do, a mac.

Silence.

(*To himself.*) Repeal and No Surrender, he says.

(*Suddenly, like a first realisation.*) Food! Food, isn't it we need?

Brian   Oh, not the greens.

Liam   If we got chance of a sheep?

Dan   Yis!

Liam   To *eat*, Malachy.

Malachy   Eat or spike, what's it to me?

Brian (*holding his stomach, beginning to laugh with a pain*) But . . . But let them . . . not get the taste of mutton on you –

Dan (*laughing*) Or the smell of it on your breath itself, Brian –

Brian Or – or . . . Or they'd soon have – (*Chuckling, he doubles up in pain.*)

Dan· Or they'd soon have you dancing a hornpipe in the air!

Brian *exits quickly.*

(*Laughing.*) God help you, Brian, a mac, with the 'looseness'.

Silence.

John Are ye thinking?

Dan Oh, we are, Johnny, we are.

Mickeleen (*muttering*) What's it to Malachy Mór, the rover.

Malachy (*to himself*) Chris-jays!

John Do you want a speak, Michael?

Mickeleen I do, I do. There's a look of a sheep to Dougan there: a ram, I'd say, the way he's eyeing Maeveen.

Liam Ary, give over.

Dan (*laughs*) Cripes, Mickeleen, if you had a body on you at all! 'Jesus shed his blood', says he.

John Ar, Danny!

Dan (*laughing*) But there's no use running your head again' a wall, perticly a church wall!

John Stop, Danny.

Dan   Sure, all I'm saying is the priests are worse off nor ourselves and we'll get nothing there.

John   I was wondering, maybe the Agent.

Liam   I was thinking of him for a job.

Dan   . . . A job with Simmington, is it?

Liam (*angrily*)   Well, if there's nothing else.

Dan   To go evicting people for him is it?

Liam (*angrily*)   Well what do *ye* say?

Dan   Tumbling houses on your neighbours for him, is it?

Liam (*angrily*)   Well, what do *ye* say? What do *ye* say we can do?

John   No, what I was saying, what I was thinking, us all go down to him and explain. To allow us time for the rent money.

Dan   And hasn't he the rent demands out already? And persons flying from them. And upwards on a thousand 'round the Lodge gates, night and day, and sorry the satisfaction any of them is getting, but a crack of the coachman's whip, for fear they'd touch the carriage, and maybe pass on a fever.

John   Oh, I don't class every man as bad at all as ye do. Simmington is a civil man enough.

Dan   Well, aren't you the changed boy, Johnny.

John   'Hat?

Dan   The head of the bull, boys, the hind-quarters of the mule, and the smile of an Englishman!

John (*angrily*)   Sure, there's only one answer to everything in the back of yere minds, but ye won't convince me.

Liam   What?

Dan   Hah?

John   If we got time for the rent – If we could use the rent money. And some of us had extra expenses this year, and maybe haven't enough to pay it – Oh, carry on!

Liam   Hah?

John (*angrily*)   Well, we'll withstand it!

Dan   Sure, we'll have to.

Liam   But how?

John   Yis!

Liam   What?

John   Aye!

Liam   Hah?

John   Wait on.

Liam   For what? Hah? You said a plan.

John   Yis, I said – Yis – I – That's what I – *we'll withstand it!* (*Turns angrily on* **Mother** *who is stirring the pot.*) What are you foosthering at it there for? You're knocking the good out of it with your poking. Coinnigh amach uaidh! (*Stand back from it! To himself.*) There's more ways to live besides food, and it's not yere way.

Brian *enters.*

Mickeleen (*to himself*)   Vastardeens and spailpeens.

Malachy (*restraining himself*)   Chris-jays! (*To* **John**.) If we had guns is it?

John   For what?

Malachy   Chris-jays, for what!

John   Yis for what?

Brian   Oh, that's all done away with now.

John   Is it that we're not dying fast enough for them? Always back to the same thing, always the same answer.

Malachy   Lord, the Connors is getting very saintly of late.

John   'Hat? Wouldn't you live for a year on the price of a gun? Wouldn't it pay your rent?

Malachy   Pikes then, sticks, and get the Cosackbawn men above with us.

John   And where will it get us now?

Brian   . . . Oh, the Cosackbawns is cute.

Dan   They're well able to go up there, Brian.

Brian   They'll be alright.

Malachy   Chris-jays, ye're talking!

John   Yis, we're talking!

Malachy   Well, tell me then whose fault is it? (*They do not appear to understand. He waves his arms about his head.*) Whose fault? All the – Why? – All over – The corn – Poor people, strangers – All over the country – Why, all over, whose fault?

Brian   Oh, sure –

Malachy   Naaw! Ye're talking. (*Pointing at* **Mickeleen**.) And the polotician there: and he's blaming me. And I know what ye're saying about me too.

Mickeleen   'Tis the sheeps' fault!

Malachy   What? . . . 'Tis! 'Tis the sheeps' fault, 'tis!

He swings and kicks out at **Mickeleen**. **Mickeleen** *retreats;* **Malachy** *pushes him out of the house.* **Mickeleen** *stays outside the house, taking shelter somewhere from the cold until the end of the scene.*

Malachy   Keep on trying me now and I'll give you what I gave you last week! (*He returns to the others.*) And if I did spike them sheep – and stakes through their sides and into the ground – And I'll spike a dozen more – But it's better nor yere moaning.

John You're getting the right to talk now, Malachy, and only that. And I'm giving you the right: remember that too.

Malachy Tell me then whose fault?

John The blight.

Malachy Naaw!

John The blight – the blight!

Malachy Naaw! Nor do you believe that. Nice homecoming from England I had: me mother and father dead, the house tumbled and the holding gone. And when there's nothing, ye're blaming me. There's no blame or shame on me. I went off to England to gather enough to get on top of the rent. He (**Liam**.) went with me, and stayed away as long, and there's no one blaming him. I dragged piaties out of that holding – out of the rocks – good years and bad. And the two bad years ye're talking about! Ary yis!

John Fight what?

Malachy That's it! That's what I'm asking.

Liam The soldiers is it?

Malachy The – soldiers – is – it, yis – is – it, ate them if you like!

John I'm not listening to ye at all. Carry on.

John *motions them to continue, that he is not interested.*

Brian Oh now, the soldiers don't do much on us indeed.

Malachy They're there!

Dan Hah?

Liam Us? The thousands of them?

Malachy   Not soldiers then – Soldiers! – Anyone! I –
know – we – can't – them – all! Some of them. One now,
and maybe two after a while as we get better. But make
such a job of that one he'd count for ten.

Dan (*excited*)   Yis! We could, we could!

Liam (*excited*)   John? John? – Hah?

John   I'm not listening to ye at all.

Dan (*looks at* **John** *and* **Brian**. *He starts to chuckle*)   . . .
We'd fight one time, but we were better fed. Suidhe síos
(*Sit down.*) Malachy, a chuid. You're stout. And all the
O'Learys were ever in it were stout.

Brian   They were.

Dan   Well, they were . . . (*Feeling sorry for* **John**.) And all
the Connors.

Brian   Well, they were.

Silence.

Mother (*apologetically; giving hint to leave*)   It's late,
Danny.

Dan   Hah? (*Then sympathetically.*) You're alright, Sinéad;
we understand, a gradh. (*The others rise with him.*) We can
be talking tomorrow. We'll have the conversation
whatever, boys.

John (*suddenly, angrily*)   And do ye think they'll get the
better of me? I'm telling ye now, so I am! (*Misinterpreting
their standing up.*) 'Hat? Sit! Ye'll heed me!

Brian   We will as always, John.

John   See if ye'll live by yere bitterness or yere fight this
time against them.

Liam   But what do you say we should do?

John   I say – I say – Something useful to be doing
until . . .

Liam   Until what?

John   Until *help* comes! Help, yis, help, that's it. Help will come, it will come, it will have to come if we give them no excuse not to send it.

Liam   But they swept the country bare today: do you think they'll refill it?

John   What else is there?! – No, what I'm saying is, last year wasn't as bad as this year is to be and they sent meal to parts.

Liam   But I think they do begrudge doing the likes and do be in no hurry.

Brian   Oh yis, the polocy.

John   But won't they have to send it to all over this year? The ways we are. They'll have to, because there's nothing else.

Liam   But when?

John   Soon. It'll depend on – Important things. The Government, the Deal, the Policy, Business – The Policy.

Brian   Oh yis.

Liam   Politicians, far away.

John   Yis, far away now, but – It wasn't given to us to understand. A bitter man or a hungry man, or a dying man doesn't understand. But they're there, and for our good, and it's better we understand that. They have rules that they must follow, and we have one: to live and be as much at peace as we can with them, as with God. (*He pauses. Then, defiantly.*) Well that's what I believe. I believe that. Help will come, because it's right. And what's right must be believed in if we're to hope. And there's nothing to be gained by listening to the contrary if we're to live at all in times like these.

Silence.

Mother   It's late.

Dan   We'll be off.

Mother   May God go with ye now.

John   What? . . . (*He realises why they are standing.*) Sit – sit
– sit. We'll all have a share. No one ever went hungry from
the house of a Connor. Sit, and don't offend us. (*To*
Mother.) We're only sorry to be able to offer so little.

Mother   'Tisn't the sweetest smelling –

John   'Hat?

Mother   . . . But there's nourishing in it. Sit. (*They sit.*)
'Tisn't too much cooked, but 'twill last longer in the
stomach that way. (*She turns on* **Maeve** *and* **Donaill** *who
have come up around the fire.*) Clear back out of my sight and
don't be looking in the mouths of people!

Malachy *moves towards the door.*

John   Malachy, I understand what you're saying, but it's
not the time.

Malachy   We'll all look out for ourselves then?

John   No.

Malachy   We all know our own know then?

John   No. You can stay the night by the hearth if you
will.

Malachy   The blight took only half the food.

Malachy *exits.*

Mickeleen (*who has been crouched at the gable-end of house,
rises; following* **Malachy**)   Vastards, the big men. But
they'll soon be a reduction. And I'll live in spite. I'll live in
spite of all.

Mickeleen *exits.*

Dan Let them off. They'll be following each other 'round all night, roaming the hills, and not speaking till they start drawing kicks on each other.

Liam . . . But there must be *some one thing* at least we can do? Until what you say, John.

Mother *allows a suitable pause for the men to come up with a suggestion; then.*

Mother There's a pile of auld boards outside the back. Couldn't ye, before someone else starts it, band together and make coffins and maybe sell them to the countryside.

Dan (*pleased*) Yis. They'll be in demand. They will.

John Take up the pot.

Dan You have a head on you, Sinéad, you have, God bless it! The meeting is closed, boys.

Scene Four

The Love Scene

A few weeks later. Night. A wood.

Occasional moonlight through the rolling clouds. A shaft of light falls on a bush. Under the bush, the corpses of a woman and her two children. A little away from them, the body of a man lying on the ground. It grows darker. The man groans. **Liam** *enters furtively. He roots under a bush on the opposite side of the stage. He produces a bag from the hole he has dug. He takes a handful of nuts and an apple from the bag. He buries the bag again. A second groan.* **Liam** *gasps. He is about to run when he hears footsteps approaching from another direction. He hides.*

Maeve *enters. Her harshness, in the early part of the scene, would be more suited to a bitter old hag.*

Liam, *hiding, makes an owl-hooting sound, a curlew whistle . . .*

Maeve *stops for a moment, looks around defiantly, is about to move again.*

Liam   There you are, Maeveen!

Maeve (*harsh*)   Mickeleen Cam!

Liam   Hillo-Hillo-Hillo?

Maeve   The huncy pleb!

Liam   Hillo-Hillo-Hillo!

Maeve   'Tis not! . . . Malachy?

Liam   'Tis a gintleman – You scoundrel – How dare you – Good evening!

Maeve   Shleeker!

Liam   Hillo!

Maeve   Vastard!

She is about to move off. Another groan from the darkness.

Liam (*urgently*)   Hillo-Hillo-Hillo! Will you marry me, Maeveen?

Silence.

We have nothing to lose.

She hides somewhere. **Liam** *comes out of hiding to follow her.*

Maeve? . . . Maeve? (*She confronts him.*) . . . Hillo!

Maeve   Dougan! Sly, rotten, foxy breed!

Liam (*unsure*)   Ar, sure, go then, you childeen . . . Sure, you're only a slip . . . (*Approaching her.*) Although, I might be making a grave mistake . . . You're purty right enough: I can see that . . . but slender.

Maeve (*snarls*)   You'd fatten me!

Liam   I – I – It's a wonder you're not afeared out here alone and all sorts of creatures coming and going through the countryside. A minute ago I thought I heard a –

Maeve   What's the shleeker's business out here?

Liam   I was hoping maybe to get a glimpse of you.

Maeve   The luck is on me, as always. The vastard shleeker is a prize!

Liam   Well, what's yours?

Maeve   Oh, I was down in Quilty's house to see if they'll march to the town with my father: But they're all off to America: And I stayed with them, preparing the sea-store for the voyage.

Liam   And was there no sport in it?

Maeve   Crying and whinging when they should be laughing.

Liam (*slipping his arm about her*)   And do you tell me you couldn't find e'er a man to folly you home?

Maeve (*shakes off his arm*)   What's on yeh!

Liam   I fear you're not affectionate.

Maeve   Chris-jays, there's a lot to give me cause.

Silence.

He puts the apple in her hand. Feeling dejected he sits. He starts to crack the nuts. He is no longer paying her attentions.

She looks at the apple; she wants to be grateful; she can't.

Liam   Your sister liked me.

Maeve   It didn't stop you wandering.

Liam   . . . You look like her.

Maeve   And leaving her.

Liam   . . . I know.

Maeve   And she's well rotten now.

Liam . . . She was gentle . . . Like Malachy Mór, I meant to stay away only the one season. But the appetite I had, and the wailing that was here.

He hands her some nuts. She looks at the apple in one hand, the nuts in the other. She takes a bite of the apple.

Maeve (*a nervous, involuntary giggle*) It's sour.

She eats more of the apple. Progressively, she becomes a sixteen-year-old girl again.

. . . Was there no hunger at all in England?

Liam There was. But I seen no man die of starvation there.

Maeve . . . If I went away I wouldn't come back.

Liam Aa, you would. Though I don't know why.

Maeve I wouldn't . . . The waiting here. Waiting for what? . . . Look at the moon trying to get out, Liam . . . And the bailley and his gang came for the cow last Monday cause we hadn't it for the rent. And they were just taking the cow out of the yard when the rates man came with his demand. And, the wind up, the bailley and the rates man were nearly coming to blows over whose right it was to the cow. And my father trying to make peace between them. (*Laughing.*) The cow just munching grass.

Liam (*beginning to laugh with her*) And who got the cow in the end?

Maeve The bailley, cause he came first . . . The cow just munching away for herself . . . Infidel and dirty and all as Mickeleen is, he's clever too. But now, my father saying we'll march to the town, legal, and explain to them, so they'll hurry up sending us meal. Will you march?

Liam . . . I got a job from the Agent today. (*He looks at her, afraid of what her reaction will be.*)

Maeve You'll get bread every day.

Liam   He's recruiting a gang: I don't know what for.

Maeve (*continues eating*)   Oh Lord, I envy Peggy Quilty off in the morning, and we're to be here waiting, and rooting over the same old fields.

Liam   What else could I do? He gave me the job because he said he never had anything against my father.

Maeve   My father saying something good will happen soon.

Liam   And I overheard them saying the word 'demolition'.

Maeve   And saying we'd be different people if someone came along and put the bit in our mouths.

Liam   There's no one thing else I can do.

Maeve   And my mother saying what's coming over my father, and saying he's soft. And I think the same. And I do be watching him thinking. And I do be wondering what does he be thinking about. And my mother saying the only things sowed anymore will be in the graveyard. And there's something coming over her. And I do hear her going out in the middle of the night with the turf basket and coming home and lying down again at dawn, cold and wet from the dew. And never seeing her shiver. But she got flour for a basket of turf the other day and the belly on Donaill swole after. (*She laughs.*) And I thought of Nora Reilly that swole and died after drinking the sup of milk . . . And I want my father to let *me* go, but he won't.

Liam   Where?

Maeve   But I think I might go myself.

Liam   Where would you go to?

Maeve   America.

Liam   Where would you get the ticket money?

Maeve   Oh, I'd snake on to one of them numerous ships and hide.

Liam (*laughs*)   They'd ketch you and drown you.

Maeve   Let them then, and I'd pray for their forgiveness while they were about it.

Liam   Well, you're an awful girl.

Maeve   I might be.

Liam   Y'are.

Maeve   And you're a fox.

Liam   Did you ever kiss a fox?

Maeve   No. And I don't want –

He pounces on her. He kisses her.

Liam   You're purty right enough. . . . Did you ever kiss anyone that was in England?

Maeve   Once only. (*He kisses her.*) Twice. (*He kisses her again.*) Three times.

They laugh. He starts to sing. She joins in singing with him.

Liam   As I roved over on a Summer's morning,
            A-speculating most curiously,
            To my surprise, whom did I espy,
            But a charming fair one approaching me;
            I stopped a while in deep meditation,
            Contemplating what I should do,
            Till at last recruiting all my sensations,
            I thus accosted the fair Colleen Rua.

Are you Aurora or the Goddess Flora,
Artemidora or Venus bright –

Through the above the moon has come out again, revealing the corpses of the family under a bush. A groan from the prone figure of the man. **Liam** *and* **Maeve** *move apart.*

Maeve (*whispers*)   Chris-jays!

Maeve *runs off.*

Liam *sees the corpses of the family and stands there as if transfixed by them.*

Scene Five

The Relief Committee

A few nights later. A room in the Town Hall. The Relief Committee is seated around a table: **Clancy**, *a merchant;* **Captain Shine**, *a landlord; Mr Simmington,* **Agent** *for an absentee landlord;* **PP** (*Parish Priest) Father Daly;* **Fr Horan**; *and* **JP** (*Justice of the Peace) who is acting Chairman.*

In the street outside, crowds are calling for 'Food! Food! Food' and 'Work! Work! Work'.

JP   I'm sorry to say we still have had no reply to the presentment we made to His Excellency, the Lord Lieutenant, to begin public works to relieve this appalling distress which God has chosen to inflict on us. Whether we presented for too much work, or whether the process of examining our application is such a slow one, I don't know. I have written to them daily stressing the urgency of our needs. I have asked them could we start on part of the work now. I have myself drawn up the plans for building a new road and submitted a copy to them and asked could we start on that . . . (*He gestures despairingly.*) . . . We are not being treated fairly. I'm sorry. I'm at a loss.

PP   Food supplies?

JP   No. They still say no. Trade must be protected. They're treating this as if it were some minor upset. I did receive that pile of government pamphlets and I have examined them, but they are totally inconsequential since we cannot eat them. I don't blame them out there, I don't blame them at all. Have you any proposals, gentlemen?

Agent   Well, the Captain and I –

Captain   Perhaps our Catholic friend, the merchant, Mr Clancy, could suggest something?

Clancy (*mutters*)   I don't know.

PP   Well, I don't know what you're doing on this committee.

Captain   Looking after your own interests, Mr Clancy? Seeing that the free-trade guarantee the Government has given you is not violated, hmm?

PP   Isn't it a great pity all the landowners wouldn't meet and see what they could do?

Agent   But that's exactly what the Government wants us to do.

PP   Yes?

Agent   But, I think, your reverence, when you hear our proposal –

Captain   No, wait, Simmington.

PP   If ye meet ye'd admit the responsibility is it?

Captain   You think the responsibility is ours?

Fr Horan   Ye own the whole country.

Captain   I'm quite aware of the limits of your thought: 'the wealthy tyrant landlord'.

Agent (*attempting a joke*)   I believe we're held responsible for the bad weather.

PP   No, Mr Simmington, we all know that the Government causes that.

JP   Gentlemen –

Captain   Well, I suggest you start pointing your finger at them for a change, or at yourselves.

PP   If that's your proposal, Captain, we'll bear it in mind.

JP   You have some – any – proposal, Captain? Mr Simmington?

Captain   Father Daly? . . . We wanted first to see what suggestions the representatives of the great Papist majority could come up with for the country . . . Well, I have talked with Simmington here and he has contacted his absent employer, and we have arranged to borrow £10,000 between us and make it available to the tenantry on our respective estates.

JP   Oh, my dear Captain –

Captain   We have arranged to *borrow* this money.

PP (*not taking bait*)   I'm sure you deserve every credit, Captain, and when we hear how you propose to spend it –

Captain   But that the 'wealthy tyrant' has to borrow! Aren't you surprised? Our Papist friends are so informed about the wealthy tyrant's side of things in their speeches and sermons and letters to the press.

JP   Ah – well – ah – (*He looks at* **PP** *to reply.*)

PP   You seem to want to talk, Captain, and since you're going to borrow the money, and if you think it's the right time –

Captain   Do you know anything about the law of entail, Daly? Or encumbrances? Or do you only know about 'the industrious but oft-abused tenantry' causing that din up and down the town out there?

Agent (*wanting to restrain him*)   Captain –

Captain   I can say with all sincerity that I have done as much honest toil in my life as any man. All I expected was fair play – from the Government and from my tenants. But the Government's imagination goes no further than rates. Aw, but the oft-abused tenantry are more resourceful. They have their feast-days and pattern days and celebrating-misery-days. The weeds must be allowed to thrive and flower and blow across on to the crops of the

industrious. There *is* a particular minority *sect* in this
community that responds to encouragement, but they, like
myself, must suffer the nettles, sorrel, docks –

Fr Horan   The present food of your tenantry.

Captain   Is that why they grow them? . . . How many
lambs blinded by the thistles every year? And did you ever
try to get an honest day's work out of one of them? And
their times of sowing: a month after the proper time. Not
for want of encouragement. But why not publish these
facts? The superstitions and witchery, fences and walls to
be knocked. How many sheep spiked wantonly every year?
Would you expect it of the black man? Ignorance, deceit,
rent evasion, begging. This county alone would furnish all
England with beggars. Filth, the breeding of disease. But,
are they so naturally this way – so naturally destructive?
Hmm? And the scrawls on the grubby little bits of paper,
threatening the life of the landlord or his wife.

Fr Horan   Well, I can tell you –

PP (*restraining him*)   Father Horan.

Captain   What can *you* tell any man? I, too, could be off
in 'the gaming houses of Europe'.

PP   Your would-be assassins are in more imminent
danger, Captain.

JP   } Gentlemen, if we could –
Captain } But are they so *naturally* this way, Daly?

PP   You're not the worst of them, Captain.

Captain   I admire – I admire – your composure, Daly.
Coming in here this evening I passed some of their pig-sty
dwellings and the chimneys are gone. I insisted all houses
have chimneys. But the chimneys are gone, the chimneys
are knocked down and the holes blocked up. What for? Is
it that the fairies don't like heights? Or was the banshee
getting caught up in them in her frequent entrances and
exits, or was it the Pope?

Fr Horan   The rents were ruz because of the chimneys!

PP   Father Horan!

Captain   Travesties of the beautiful countryside.

Fr Horan   And the houses were cold because of them.

PP   Father Horan! I agree with a lot you say, Captain.

Captain   Of course. You can't deny it here.

PP   It will be a slow process.

Captain   Yes, there's a slow process in operation. And we've grown soft.

JP   Please, could we, perhaps, get back to –

Fr Horan   It's just that you don't understand the Irish yet.

Captain   What?! But I am Irish, stupid priest! And don't speak until you are spoken to. You are not a member of this committee. Or I wasn't consulted about your co-option if you are. My family goes back several hundred years.

Fr Horan   To some time of conquest, no doubt, *your honour*.

Captain   Yes? But I didn't steal your land, boy.

Fr Horan   It was stolen, it was stolen! And time won't make the theft right.

Captain   It seems I've committed a felony. I'm the receiver of stolen goods. Must I give it back?

Fr Horan   I didn't say – Yes! Yis! Yis!

Captain   To primitive man?

Fr Horan   To the people! To the people!

PP } Father Horan!
JP } Gentlemen!

Captain   This is, indeed, a strange country: There are Irish and Irish who aren't Irish.

Fr Horan   Yis! – Great Irish! – Who will yet legislate for themselves!

Captain } Is there a –
PP   } Father Horan!
Fr Horan } The Union will be repealed!
JP   } Gentlemen, please, I must ask you –

Captain   Is there a pure Irish race somewhere, or are you referring to the monkeys roaming the hills out there? Monkeys who could now be men, but for the popery that keeps them apart!

Fr Horan   We can wait! We won't forget the past! Your breed will go! You'll see!

Captain   There it is! That's what I wanted to hear!

PP   Father Horan, I forbid you to say another word!

Captain   There it is! They can wait! There's their slow process! Do they want to be helped, are they so naturally evil, or is there some cunning power directing all this, some malicious conspiracy, directed by the Roman anti-Christs that would have the well-meaning robbed and reduced to squalor and filth on a level with their own.

PP (*to* **Fr Horan**)   You have a lot of sick calls to make. I don't think you should waste your time here. Tell them outside to pray.

Fr Horan *leaves*.

Well, Captain, you bought the right, and now, if you've got your pound of flesh, maybe we can –

Captain   No, sir! I thought it was timely to let you know that we are aware of what's going on.

PP   Fair enough. Just, it struck me more like the babbling of a drowning man.

Captain   No, sir! No, sir! And half the countries of the world have been conquered as long ago as Ireland has, and conqueror and conquered have managed to work together and prosper without any fine-cut distinctions of nationality or unending vicious conspiracy.

PP   There's no conspiracy: I'm not going arguing nonsense with you. But I'll say one thing, the fine-cut distinctions you talk about might be due to the fact that men like you still behave like conquerors – No-no-no, Captain – Listen, I'll be off too if I'm only hampering the real business of the meeting. I'll call later to the Chairman and –

JP   For heaven's sake, gentlemen, please! Could we be seated again.

Fr Horan (*off; calling to crowd*)   Kneel! Kneel! . . . Now, pray! Pray! (*Hushed murmuring of prayers.*)

JP   . . . To remind you, gentlemen, that yesterday, a whole family was found dead in a wood about seven miles from here. No one knows who they are or where they came from. At this moment there are seven or eight funerals waiting outside the cemetery . . . Could we hear your proposal or plan, Captain?

Agent   Perhaps, Captain, if *I* outlined what we have in mind . . . (*He smiles at meeting, the most amiable of men.*) It's a simple little plan, gentlemen. Well, as the Captain said, the country must be saved no matter what the cost. Now, the way we see the situation is this. Are we to receive relief in the form of food supplies from our free-trade, or free-for-all, government? No. Can we expect permission to begin public works? Yes. *Sometime* in the future. But even with the sanctioning of Public Work, will the building of a road or a wall absorb half the labour force around here or fill one quarter of the bellies? Well now, what else have we? Yes, we hear of the charitable organisations and we know of the costly, dangerous and unselfish nature of their administration, but what can they hope to achieve against

such odds of numbers? Indeed, many people maintain –
and dare I disagree? – that well-meaning though these
organisations might be, the fact remains that alms-giving is
contrary to the spirit of industry we should like to see
fostered in this country. But that is just a by-the-way.

Clancy   Hear – hear!

JP   What is your proposal, Mr Simmington?

Agent   The Captain and I are pointing out that all doors
seem to be closed on us, and that –

PP   What is your plan, Mr Simmington?

Agent   All this, your reverence, to avoid wasting time on
possible argument later on.

PP (*suspicious*)   What?

Agent   Can any thinking man, your reverence, seriously
believe that we can hope for constructive help in the
immediate future from our Government?

PP   Yes, yes, but, what do you propose to do?

Agent   It was only the other day I was saying to Captain
Shine that I should like to say we are dealing with *faction*
politics, not party politics. That at the moment one faction
in the Commons is saying there is no distress here: that
that belief has come from the famed Irish imagination.
While another faction says we've got *famine* here, but of
such magnitude that it is impossible for them to deal with
it. And yet another: that if we have a problem, it's ours, we
created it, and solve it we must alone; that they are sick
and tired of dependent Ireland; that we have arrived at
the stage, they say – humorously – where an Irish
gentleman cannot marry off his daughter without first
seeking the advice and aid of Government. But I must
mention one last group. I speak objectively, and with all
due respect to any individual's political leanings. The Irish
MPs of O'Connell's party. The statements of this group
amount to the belief that if the people starve patiently the

result will be a speedier repeal of the Union between Great
Britain and Ireland.

PP   Very good, Mr Simmington, now how do you
propose to spend this money?

Agent   I'm coming to it, your reverence.

PP   How will you import speedily enough such large
quantities of food to –

Captain   What?

Agent   Well, your reverence, we think it may not be a
question of importing food.

PP   What?

Agent   You see, what we first of all tried to make our
Government see is the recurring hopelessness here when all
the while prosperity is there for the taking in other parts of
the world.

PP   What? – For who? – What are you saying?

Captain   He's saying, Daly –

Agent   I'm saying, your reverence, the world is opening
out. New continents with untold natural wealth are
waiting to be reclaimed by the brave pioneer hand –

PP   Food! Soup! Meal! –

Agent   Huge tracts of land waiting to be tilled, to
produce food, unlimited food for everyone. A new world
that promises –

PP   Clear them is it?

Agent   No.

PP   What then?

Agent   Aid them to emigrate.

PP   This is what ye worked out?!

Captain   We are prepared to spend –

PP   Yes, Captain, ye are prepared to spend. If I had known the measure of your scheme ye would not have made your fine humbug speeches. Ye had no right. Indulging yourselves in your high-fallutin' ráimeis that showed up your hypocrisy and ignorance as much as your arrogance.   .

Captain   I'm afraid I don't understand your attitude.

PP   I'm sure you don't!

Agent   Your reverence –

PP   I didn't think you would. You're not Irish! – You're not Irish!

Captain   What can you offer them?

PP   What can I offer them? You – you talk about new continents, land to be reclaimed, and not a farthing to clear a stick or a stone off all the land that lies about ye here in a state of nature. Not a farthing piece to drain a drop of water off all the acres and acres of bog.

Agent   We're offering a great number of people an alternative to death.

PP   And we've been watching the tricks of the *adventurer* too, Mr Simmington, this while back, agent, or part-owner, or whatever you are now of your absent employer's estate.

JP   I see merit in the scheme.

PP   Well, there's a smell off the merit. (*Turns on* **Captain**.) Yes, Shine – Yes, Shine, they're poor people, ignorant, demoralized and dirty, moulded and shaped that way by England and by England's tools, the landlords, over the past five or six hundred years. Colonization and poverty! And all we can see after all those centuries of British rule and justice is a Union flag flying proud over an empty government meal depot up the road there and a mob of howling peasants around it.

JP We understand, Father Daly, but we must think of the moment now. It's a solution.

PP Clear them! Get rid of them! And that's the extent of relief that can be offered in this modern year of 1846?

JP Large numbers are emigrating voluntarily, so to speak.

Agent Oh, there's no question of compulsion.

JP No – no, of course not.

PP (*to* **Clancy**) Have you anything at all to say, Clancy? Didn't you make fortune enough last year? Is there any spirit in you at all other than greed that would make you close down your whiskey houses and throw open your big stores now, instead of waiting for starvation prices to soar higher?

Agent Your reverence –

PP What are ye addressing this at me for?

Agent What else can be offered them?

Captain What can *you* offer them?

PP (*viciously*) A captain, a captain! And sure little schoolboys with any background get that rank straightaway on entering the army! (*He turns away, wincing at his own malice.*)

Agent Father Daly –

PP Well, I have faith in humanity! – I have faith in – What are ye addressing this at me for?

Agent Well, frankly, the unfortunate relationship that has grown up between landlord and tenant.

PP In spite of yere gentle encouragement . . . Aaa, I see, now! And ye need the help of the clergy in clearing a reluctant peasantry off the land they were born in and love?

Agent . . . Well, if you insist on putting it that way.

PP (*a last try*) Would nothing induce ye to spend the money here?

Agent It's not a matter of spending the money here. Common sense. It's getting worse every year: This tillage system is hopeless: The country is a workhouse.

PP But this great sum. Couldn't it be used for –

Captain Rates cost us more yearly.

PP . . . Rates cost ye more?

Agent (*forcing a laugh, trying to cover the blunder*) Yes, who would have thought?

PP It's cheaper to clear them! . . . *Who* are we saving?

Agent It may not appear obvious now, but it's the only hope for the country.

PP turns away from them.

Short silence.

JP Well . . . I feel . . . I think . . . Have you decided on a?

Captain Canada.

JP And when do you think?

Agent It will take a month to complete arrangements.

JP Do you intend the offer for a particular class?

Agent No. It's to be a general offer, though, generally – I mean naturally – the most needy will get preference.

JP And I expect a number of those who might accept have leases or made improvements: do you propose to?

Captain What?

JP Would you compensate them?

Captain   Good God, man, you might as well propose compensating the rabbits for digging holes in the ground! I've never seen half of them before.

JP   How many do you propose to – to – to emigrate?

Agent ⟩ Two thousand.
Captain ⟩ Three thousand.

JP   . . . I see.

Short silence.

Agent (*forces a laugh*)   But, though neither am I of the Catholic Church, it was only the other day that I thought that emigration – and such as we propose – could be considered a means towards spreading that faith throughout the world. Though, I think better of mentioning it now. But still.

PP   Not bad, Mr Simmington, but I'm not as naive as you think . . . I did think a minute ago of something in its favour. (*He looks at* **Clancy**.) Your scheme would relieve those poor people out there of all sight and dealings with the accursed gombeen man whose fate, I feel certain, is more assured than the fate of Judas. (*He turns away again, wincing at his own words.*) . . . But I think now of the long sea voyage, in the ships that are coming to be known as coffinships. And at the end of the journey, opportunity, maybe. But I see them, a herd of innocents, starved and diseased, thrown up on a foreign shore, the sacrificial offerings of a modern world. This prosperous Christian world. I wonder is there another part of the world today stricken like ourselves? And I wonder is there a body of leaders, principled men, believing in an ideal for the world and letting a great chance go by. Because this is an opportunity, and the leaders should be rushing forward to grasp it with all the love and help they've got to further the hope of the ideal. Otherwise, better stop talks of ideals entirely and say that life is based on a lie; otherwise, what can be expected of evolving man. (*The others are showing signs of impatience.*) If it was needed for a war against the

Afghans! But, maybe I've been a simple old fool all my life.
Maybe economies can only survive and cater for the
catastrophe of war. Ye're impatient, gentlemen.

Agent   Time.

PP   Yes, time is against us too. And I have no answers.
But the future will answer us all.

JP   Well, I suggest, that perhaps the best thing to do
would be to interview them individually. That is when
you've gone further with your preparations.

Agent   But it would be – nice – if we could tell them
something tonight.

JP   Well, perhaps, if they were told generally about the
scheme now.

Agent   Certainly.

JP   It would give them time to be thinking about it.

Agent   Excellent. Would Fr Daly like to address them?
(**PP** *shakes his head.*)

Captain   But, surely to God, man, you can't tell them to
refuse?

PP   If we could at least keep God's name out of it.
Consider only that I'm not your enemy. The decision will
have to be theirs.

Scene Six

The Quarry

A few weeks later. A rise overlooking a quarry. Night.

A rabbit cooking over a small fire. **Malachy** *has collected a pile of
stones. He weighs one of them in his hand. He carries them off, and
returns with an armful of twigs which he places in readiness beside
the fire. His movements are deliberate; an air of cool and ruthless
detachment about him. He hears a noise off. He hides.*

Mickeleen *enters and waits.* **Malachy** *reappears; he realizes that the errand he has sent* **Mickeleen** *on has not been successful.* **Mickeleen** *laughs. Though his speeches are bitter and taunting, he is wary of* **Malachy**.

Mickeleen   They won't come up . . . I say the scarecrows won't come up to visit you. They have lots to be doing. Still talking about the emigration: Connor wondering is it right to take it. Hah, Seán? . . . And I told them you'd have a sheep for them to eat. (*He laughs.*) But they doubted even Malachy Mór'd manage to steal one and all the bodacks of guards Simmington has. And, for why, they asked, did you pick a place on the rise beside the quarry for a meeting and chance catching a fever from one of the workhouse paupers buried ablow. On that account, I said, 'twould be safest from the peelers. But the fire cooking it, they said, would of a certainty be sure to be seen by the peelers patrolling the glen and they'd have to drop in on us. (*Laughs.*) But to thank you kindly . . . Christ, a noble plan to trick your army up here.

Malachy (*quietly*)   Eat, Michael.

Mickeleen *takes a piece of the rabbit. He starts to kick some ashes on the fire to damp it down,* **Malachy** *growls, then starts to kindle it.*

Mickeleen   Ara what? . . . And they were talking about Liam Dougan too as is now a top bodack of a vastard for Simmington. And they're sorry for Brian Riordan because some thief has all his turf near stolen, all to the few ciaráns. Hah, I said, maybe the dispossessed Learys took it? The small bandy cripple and his brother of the great stature that's handy at the deserting. The Learys is bad, I said; they'd take a snail from a blind hen, I said . . . (*Notices fire is brightening up.*) Not that I fear any parish tyrant of a rotten peeler – We're doing no harm – but if they come up here now and remember me – cause I'm easy remembered – from the day of the corncarts.

Malachy (*putting sticks on the fire; to himself*)   Ar yis, yis, yis, yis, yis.

Mickeleen (*looking into quarry*)   The wind blowing down there – Curse of Christ! Curse of Christ! – going astray in its direction blowing, throwing all classes of rotten fevered paupers' diseases up on top of us. (*Glances at the brightening fire again.*) And the peelers too is looking for some gallant rebel that stoned to death the soldier's horse that used be straying at night.

Malachy (*quietly; looking into quarry*)   Lime, Michael, the quick-lime: it burns them, diseases and all: the paupers, and the odd stray one they pick up dead in the fields.

Mickeleen   Connor, I said, Seán, I said, don't you reckon they'd have blessed the smaller quarry in Clonshee if they expected your sort of help to come. (*Suddenly soft.*) Connor. The meal will come. Johnny Connor. (*Suddenly harsh again.*) Seán! – Vastard! – Pleb! – Lúdramán! – He'd make a one seafóideach with his class of talk!

Malachy   Over there, wasn't it, Tomás and Mary Leary rotted on the hillside, yourself in attendance, Michael, this time last year?

Mickeleen (*looking into quarry again*)   I often heard tell of one being buried alive. How many would you say to fill it?

Malachy *moves off, looking down into the glen.*

Mickeleen (*nervously, to himself*)   Ara what? . . . You'll not clear your conscience this night! You'll not –

Malachy *enters.*

Malachy   But 'twas a good plan, Michael. I thought to myself, since Connor is scattered, myself to be leader. Five men, cripples or no, would have done easy. (*Pointing to where he would have positioned them.*) One there, one behind the boulder, one in the hollow yonder against the furze, myself there on the ledge in the quarry, and yourself running, making enough noise for us all. The peelers

hearing you would stop there. They don't expect revenge.
And we'd have two guns, the start of an army to see whose
fault.

A noise off. **Malachy** *motions* **Mickeleen** *to be quiet, and he
moves off cautiously to investigate the noise.*

Mickeleen   . . . Ara what? Ara what? . . . Fine plan, fine
plan – Christ! The big stature. And deserting us again
tomorrow. Like the other vastards and spalpeens. Go, let
ye, one way or the other. My name is on no list for going.
Show yere bodies to the world. Hop a stone off a man's
head and ye're free. And the cripple is left to all these
ghosts and the hills.

Malachy *enters.*

Malachy   Whist! They're coming. When I give you the
word –

Mickeleen   Ara what?

Malachy   Stand still till I give you the word. Then make
noise running as if – (*He grabs at* **Mickeleen**.)

Mickeleen (*dodges him*)   Ara what? Christ! Ara what?

Mickeleen *escapes and runs off.*

Malachy *stands motionless for a moment. The police can be heard
apparoaching.* **Malachy** *starts to mutter to himself, his
determination beginning to falter.*

Malachy   Chris-jays . . . Chris-jays . . . Chris-jays.

*He starts to run, in several directions, growing confused. He kicks
ashes on the fire and races off.*

First *and* **Second Policeman** *enter. They wait, until the
fading noises of* **Mickeleen** *and* **Malachy** *are gone. They
search about the place for a few moments. Then they relax.*

First Policeman   They're well gone.

Second Policeman   Two of them, I'd say.

First Policeman   Let them keep going.

Second Policeman   A rabbit.

First Policeman (*warms his hands at fire*)   Lord, it's bitter cold, Ciarán.

Second Policeman   There's no fight in them.

First Policeman   What did we do to deserve to be out in a place like this?

Second Policeman   Be thankful to God you have a job at all.

First Policeman   Well, it's not that they're giving us much trouble. But it's bitter cold, Ciarán.

Second Policeman   There's no spark in them. Times I'm ashamed of them. I wouldn't starve so quiet, I'm telling you. And the fearful army of spectres they'd make.

First Policeman   Gobs, I'm not going to complain about that.

Second Policeman   That's what I'd like.

He goes to the quarry and looks down into it.

First Policeman (*takes a bottle from his pocket*)   Do you think it's a famine? They're saying it is. (*He takes a drink; then, philosophically.*) Oh, what can stop a famine!

Second Policeman   What's down there?

First Policeman   What can stop a famine! It's a quarry. I wish it was Spring. (*He is taking another drink.*)

Second Policeman   No, a neat pile of stones on the ledge there, like as if –

*At this moment **Malachy** rushes out of the darkness, arms outstretched. He pushes **Second Policeman** into the quarry, jumps on **First Policeman** and kills him with a stone. He takes **First Policeman**'s gun and races off.*

Scene Seven

The Interview

A week later. The rent office.

Agent *sits inside the window of the rent office, a list of names before him. On a table outside the window is a similar list for the marks or signatures of those being interviewed.* **Agent** *has a long pointer for indicating where the signatures should be made. (These precautions are taken in fear of fever contagion.)*

Liam *is outside the rent office, acting as the* **Agent**'s *usher.*

A crowd of people (on or offstage) are waiting to be interviewed.

A Man, *standing outside rent office, puts his mark on the paper that is on the table and is waved off.*

Agent   Incomprehensible, some of them. (*Adding numbers on his list.*) Six hundred and eight and six is six hundred and fourteen . . . Now, next area. Glanconor village. John Connor. He's some sort of village elder, isn't he? (**Liam** *nods.*) We'll get his acceptance first. Call him.

Liam   John Connor! . . . John Connor!

John, *now looking more dead than alive, enters and stands at the table.*

Agent   Connor. You've decided? (*He glances up at* **John**'s *abject expression and decides for himself in the affirmative.*) How many of you? – Look the other way when you speak. (**John** *obediently turns his head away from the* **Agent**.) Good man. Make sure you do not breathe in this direction. How many of you? Wife, children, grandparents.

John   Four.

Agent   Look the other way, man! . . . Four.

John   But –

Agent   Put your mark there.

John   Ah –

Agent   What?

John (*apologetically*)   I can write, your honour.

Agent   Look the other way – Look the other way! You can write. Good man. Sign there. (*Adding numbers on his papers.*) Six hundred and fourteen and four –

John   I don't know.

Agent   What?

John   If I was sure.

Agent   If you were sure.

John   I'd go if I was sure.

Agent   Oh now, my good man, I haven't to go through all this again, have I?

John (*appears to be in a daze*)   No.

Agent   Of course I can't compel you to go.

John   Yes, your honour.

Agent   What?

John   No, your honour.

Agent   I can't compel you to go.

John   No, your honour.

Agent   I can't compel you.

John   No, your honour.

Agent   Have your clergy spoken against it?

John   No, your honour.

Agent   There you are then.

John   No, your honour.

Agent   Stop! Are you listening to me at all?

John   Maybe to wait a while longer.

Agent   You're some kind of village leader aren't you? Are you possibly the man who led the Glanconor people to join that mob in town a few weeks ago?

John   To explain, your –

Agent   To explain. Well, maybe we'll forget that.

John   I'm confused.

Agent   Indeed you are. Aren't you hungry – Do you like starvation – Do you want to die in the fields – Quicker still in the workhouse – Do you want to die of fever?

John   No, your honour.

Agent   Hmm?

John   I had it once, your –

Agent   What?

John   The workhouse were built for paupers, your honour.

Agent   Yes –

John   We're farmers.

Agent   Farmers. And you should know by now that the land you hold is no good except, possibly, for grazing. All the good land waiting for you in Canada. You look a sensible man.

John   Naaw.

Agent   What?

John (*neurotically*)   Only what's right, I must do only what's right.

Agent   You want to do the right thing, of course you do –

John   Yis, your honour, only what's right –

Agent   Turn your head the other way!

John And for the Glanconors. And if you can explain, and that it's right, and explain the reason, we'll go.

Agent The reason? (*He laughs at* **John**.)

John (*first trace of defiance*) I could have gone years ago, my father could have gone, my grandfather –

Agent The reason. Aren't you starving?

John Naaw!

Agent Aren't you starving? –

John Naaw!

Agent Isn't your wife starving? Your children?

John . . . I'll look after them.

Agent Will you? . . . I think you're just being stubborn, Connor. And selfish.

John But we've been here so long. Waiting.

Agent And now help has come. Isn't this the answer to your prayers?

John If you can explain to me the reason why it is.

Agent (*losing control*) Aw, listen here – (*He controls himself, forces a laugh.*) I think I know what's wrong. You're afraid to go, afraid of the water like some of the others.

John We sowed the crop, it failed again: that's all.

Agent A big man like you. There, Connor, put your mark there.

John (*defiantly*) I can write!

Agent Now listen here – listen here – listen here – listen! Who else will help you if I don't? You're not one of those expecting government aid are you? What? Well, you can forget that.

John } That can't be. We're peaceful, we're doing no
wrong –
Agent } That can be! That is!

John   We sowed the crop, it failed again: that's all.

Agent   There will be no government aid, no aid, so who
else will assist you if I don't?

John   There's a God above still we hope.

Agent   Will He pay the rent for you, will He pay the
rates?

John   I've paid my rent! The oats! – And the cow you
took! – The cow! – And how long will the voyage take? –
And to what part of Canada? – And how many acres will
we get? – And does anyone know we're coming? – And
how hot or how cold is it there? And will there be any
compensation for –

Agent   Get back from the window, I'm not spending any
more time on you. I expected your gratitude because I am
the only one who has pity on you. You will receive help
from no other quarter – Don't shake your head! By signing
that paper you will be doing the right thing: I can assure
you it's God's will. Is that sufficient explanation for you?

John   He gave me a will too.

Agent   Alright, Connor, listen carefully. Every man of
you on my estate – *my* estate! – is a half-year's rent in
arrears –

John   Begging your pardon, but isn't that the way it
always was?

Agent   By law – by law, on that account, there isn't a
man among you I can't have out on the roadside in the
morning. I'm not going to have some staying and some
going. I'm not going to be ruined by half measures after
my years here. Do you understand that? . . . Now, sign
there.

John *looks at him.*

Turn your head the other way.

John (*does not obey*)   We'll withstand it!

Agent   Turn your head!

John   We'll live!

Agent   Look the other way!

John   I won't go.

Agent   Why? (*Shouts.*) Why? – Why? – Why?

John *keeps looking at him.* **Agent** *hits him with the pointer.*

Get back, Connor! Get away, get away!

John *walks away, much more alive than dead.*

Next! Next! O'Dea, Daniel O'Dea!

Liam   Daniel O'Dea, Daniel O'Dea! . . . Daniel O'Dea!

Agent   Dineen, Marcus Dineen!

Liam   Marcus Dineen! Marcus Dineen!

Agent   Malachy O'Leary!

Liam   Malachy O'Leary!

Agent   Riordan! Brian Riordan!

Liam   Brian Riordan! . . . Brian Riordan!

Agent   Connor, Connor, get Connor back here!

But **John** *has gone.*

If crowd is on stage, **Dan**, **Dan's Wife**, **Brian** *and*
Mickeleen *follow* **John**.

Mark *remains, waiting to accept the offer.*

Scene Eight

Albert O'Toole

John's *house and the road outside.* **Dan** *and* **Mickeleen** *are outside the door, looking off. They move in and out of the house.*

A little away from them, also looking off, are **Mother**, **Maeve** *and* **Dan**'s **Wife**.

The house is almost bare of furniture and effects. A few coffins are stacked in a corner, one of them painted red. **John** *is working doggedly on another – a coffin with a trap-bottom.* **Donaill** *is beside him.* **Brian** *sits by the fire; he remains silent throughout.*

Mickeleen (*calling*)   Hah, Seán?

Dan (*looking off*)   There's no sign of them moving yet . . . There's the widdy and her brood. (*Calls.*) Johnny! And, aw, will you look at himself! Marcusheen! . . . He's looking up this way. Pull back or he'll see you. (*They stand in the doorway.*) Johnny! . . . The crowd of them!

Mickeleen   What's the matter, Seán?

Dan   I never thought to see a Glanconor go without as much as a shake hands. Comical. (*Joins* **John**.) Yis, we must struggle on whatever. We're upset. (*Proud.*) But we refused their offer, John. We did. We did.

John   I don't understand it.

Dan   Hah? . . . (*Referring to coffin with trap-bottom.*) Oh, never fear, Johnny, this melodian will be our saviour yet. (*Pointing at red coffin.*) Wouldn't you think that would attract anyone? But, when the customer hasn't it for the real article, this contraption. And when we were only paid for three, was it? Two? Four? Hah? Oh, maith go leor, who could refuse a dead man – (*Laughs.*) or woman. The dead must be protected, if only for a time. I'd prefer the wolf any day to the rat.

John (*to himself*)   Am I doing right or wrong?

Dan (*looks at* **John**'*s work; laughs*)   Isn't it simple as life and death itself!

John (*angrily*)   Heed me!

Mickeleen (*calls*)   Don't let it best you, Seán.

John   Them is the sides nailed: Now which do I nail fast, the top or the bottom?

Dan   The bottom.

John   But didn't ye say a trap bottom? – Sure, you won't heed me! Whichever you nail fast, the open end will always have to be up to receive the corpse: but then if the open end is to be the trap bottom, you have to turn the coffin over: but then you'll be carrying them on their faces, carrying them on their faces.

Dan   Nail down the top and you'll understand. You're not working so tasty as you were. (*Goes to fire.*) There's none of us is, Brian, no, a mac. (*Surveys the bare house.*) And there's nothing left to sell – (*He laughs.*) Save, if we pawn one of the women. Are they still there, Mickeleen?

Mickeleen   Yis, na vastards!

Dan   Carney buried the wife in a bag last night. Now! And never came anear us. A person'd soon go rottening through a bag. The maggots is the boyos to the dead. But isn't the rat worse to living dead? Hah? A strange little animal. Buried Nell Carney in a bag. But, isn't it the same with this style – Lord, a chuid, style: trapdoors in coffins, a Thighearna! (*Lord!*) 'Tisn't the most natural, we know, but the journey to the graveyard, tuigeann sibh, (*Ye understand.*) to be respectable in the eyes of the world.

John   Hold it for me.

Dan (*helps* **John**)   We'd want a couple every day to struggle it out until . . . until . . . Hah? And they're in it too, if only they'd come to us.

John   Why do you keep talking?

Dan   I'm holding it . . . I'll be in that red vessel myself yet, if you don't go before me, Johnny. (*Laughs.*) Or maybe Mickeleen'd fly before any of us!

John   Why do you keep talking?

Dan   I'm holding it!

Mickeleen   Here he's up! Marcus!

Mickeleen *draws back into the house.* **Mother**, **Maeve** *and* **Dan**'s **Wife** *pull back also.* **Dan** *and* **Mickeleen** *peep out the door.*

Look at him! He thinks he's secure now! The Dineen breed, and all his breed before him! His grandfather one time that stole the spade that was the only livehood to Peadar Bane. His sister that used to give belly to the soldiers at the fairs in Turlough.

Dan   The peacock! Look at the strut of him!

Mickeleen   The dirty breed!

Dan   The Dineens how-are-yeh!

Mark *enters timidly, slowly, his eyes on the road all the while. He waits.*

John   'Hat? – Go out to him – Didn't we just refuse? Go out to him.

Mickeleen   Let the spalpeen go now.

John   Go out, can't you, Danny, bid the man adieu.

Dan   . . . Aaaa . . .

John   What's coming over ye at all?

John *comes out to* **Mark**, *followed by* **Donaill**, **Mickeleen** *and* **Dan**. **Brian**, *trance-like, follows.* **Mother**, **Maeve** *and* **Dan**'s **Wife** *approach.*

Go mbeannuighthe Dia dhuit, a Mhark! I knew you'd come up to see us before going.

Mickeleen What's delaying yere departure?

Mark A crowd above in Cosackbawn is inclined to renege and the bailley is gone up to tumble their houses and bring them down.

Mickeleen And your own will be levelled before duskess. (*Dusk.*)

Mark What's to signify in that now?

Not having an answer he looks to **John** *to supply one.*

Mickeleen Oh, we bid the deserters farewell.

John (*to* **Mark**, *gently*) You're not going alone whatever.

Mark But the ones that were nearest ever to me?

Mickeleen And Albert O'Toole will be after you.

Mark Who?

Mickeleen From Pullanoar.

Mark I don't know the man.

Mickeleen Don't you? Well, whether you do or no, he refused Simmington *and* the Captain. And Danny O'Dea there refused. And they threatened John Connor here with whips about arrears, but he wouldn't be – transported.

John Stop now! – Oh but I wouldn't go for them alright.

Mark But why are ye staying?

Mickeleen *and* **Dan** *look to* **John** *to reply.*

John (*losing control*) That's why! – That's why! – That's why!

Mickeleen And you'll be no sooner gone when the roadworks will be starting up.

John And help – the meal – it's coming, it's coming.

Mark But all that's dying.

John   Yis, but the roadworks, and – but did you hear about Albert O'Toole threatening them?

Mark   Sure, I don't know the man.

Mickeleen   Did you hear about Albert O'Toole threatening them? –

John   Did you? –

Mark   Sure, we never knew anyone from Pullanoar –

John   But did you hear – did you hear –

Mark   But Tom Fada is going and the widdy and hundreds –

John   But did you hear – (*Urging* **Dan** *to speak.*) Danny.

Mickeleen   The only journey I'll be making, says Albert O'Toole –

John⎫ He did, he did.
Dan⎭ Will be direct to hell, chasing your vile souls there.

John   He did, he did!

Dan ⎫ By the five crosses, says he –
Mark⎭ But, sure, we never knew anyone from –

Dan   By all that's before ye, behind ye, above ye, ablow ye, and all about ye –

Mark   ⎫ Sure I don't know the man.
Mickeleen⎭ I'll live to see ye transformed to dung.

Dan   And they arrested him.

John   Do you know that? –

Mickeleen   Do you, Dineen? –

Dan   Do you know that? –

Mickeleen   And do you know that when Father Daly –

Dan   The parish priest himself –

Mickeleen   Heard that the peelers had him, and his wife barely cold in her deathbed, up went his reverence and got his release for the duration of the funeral –

John   Do you know that? –

Dan   And that was maith go leor until whatever cullermuggerin' the ophans had 'round the grave as the mother was going under, but they were laughing whatever, and 'Hacka!', says Albert, hitting the eldest putack a smather and stretching him on the clay, and then off with him racing, 'cross the fields, na police air a thóir (*Chasing him.*) nor did they ketch him – No! – till he was halfway through the Lodge windy, and a lump of a stone to him to get at Simmington.

John   He'll be remembered.

Dan   He'll be remembered –

Mickeleen   There's some brave men yet –

Dan   Sure, he's a hero.

Mickeleen   A great man –

Dan   A hero –

Mickeleen   Not a bodack of a vastardeen of a deserter!

John   Stop! (*Realising he has lost control of himself.*)

Mark   But – but – but, Australia they'll send him to.

Mickeleen   Will it? –

Dan   Will it now? –

Mickeleen   It's all the same: Canada or Australia.

John   Stop.

Mark   . . . Sure I'm not happy to be leaving ye. I'd renege myself but I can't watch any more of them die on me. (*He produces his ticket.*) And they do say it's prosperous. And no dealings there with landlord or bailley. A famous

country next to America that the English has little or no to
do with.

Mickeleen   The same English is stuck everywhere.

The sight of the ticket has a quietening effect on them. **Mother**
examines it.

Mark   They'd take more yet. They'd take ye now.
There's time.

John (*conscious of* **Mother**'*s eyes on him; examining the
ticket*)   It looks legal enough.

Mark   Johnny? They'll wait an hour for ye. They'll have
ye out anyway because they're going making a grazing
range out of the whole village. They let me up so as to tell
ye.

John (*hands ticket back to* **Mark**)   You'll be alright,
Marcus, we wish you well.

John *shakes hands with* **Mark** *and returns to house, followed by*
Donaill*; he resumes working on the coffin.*

Mark *starts to cry.*

Mark   We'll be shifting anytime now . . . Oh Lord, and
I'm afeared of the water. And I had a dream. Goodbye to
ye, I'll do nothing wrong, I'll do nothing wrong. And I
dreamt Canada was at the bottom of the ocean. And some
say the captain and sailors is ojus drinkers. They won't let
herself up. To be leaving ye all. And my own childre
ablow, and what will Glanconor mean to them after six
months out of it, or the fields, or the hazel beyond . . .

He exits through the speech.

Mother, **Maeve** *and* **Dan**'*s* **Wife** *move off to watch* **Mark**'*s
departure.* **Brian** *continues motionless, standing outside, like
something forgotten.*

Dan   He was nice. Poor Marcus . . . (*As he goes into house.*)
I'd go myself but I'm too old . . . And I was counting for

herself last night, all that's gone, dead, left, or disappeared and I don't know how many I counted.

John (*finishes the coffin*) I don't understand it.

Dan You put them in the usual way, like this, and then turn the coffin over and . . . (*He sees the problem.*)

John Carrying them on their faces.

Mickeleen (*coming into house*) Hah, Seán?

Dan Maybe if you'd put the handles on the other –

Mickeleen What's the matter, Seán?

John (*turns suddenly and catches* **Mickeleen** *by the throat*) I'm standing over you now, Michael, the likely way 'twill always be: I've never afflicted you because God himself choosed you for misfortune: But don't keep on, for I'd not want to use on you the sacred strength I'll always have kept aside! (*Releases* **Mickeleen** *and turns back, glaring at the coffin.*)

Dan Just for carrying them to the graveside, sure.

John (*grabs* **Donaill** *and lifts him up*) Open it! Now which way his face?

Mickeleen Down.

John 'Hat?

Mickeleen Down! Down! And turn it over.

They put **Donaill** *into the coffin face down.*

John Close it. Put the clasp on.

Mickeleen Turn it over . . . Now he's right ways up.

John Lift it . . . Walk . . . Stop . . . Loosen the catch.

The catch is loosened and **Donaill** *tumbles out on to the floor. He stays there whimpering.* **Dan**, **Mickeleen** *and* **John** *laugh.*

Dan I knew it wouldn't best you, Johnny.

Mickeleen   'Tis fit for man, woman or child, Seán.

Dan   And a fourpence is not unreasonable for such a serious journey.

John (*lifting* **Donaill** *to his feet*)   Aw, musha, a mac, it's only a bit of sport we're having. Run down to your mother, there's mo bhuachaill. (*My boy.*)

He leads **Donaill** *outside,* **Donaill** *runs off.*

John *stands beside* **Brian** *who has remained outside since* **Mark***'s departure,* **John** *is looking off into the distance, vacantly.* **Mickeleen** *comes to* **John***'s side, looks off also, but is puzzled.*

Mickeleen   . . . But what thing is it ye're waiting for? John?

John   Not for you, *Mickeleen.*

Scene Nine

The Assassination

A few weeks later.

Liam, *the foreman on the roadworks, is walking along a stretch of new road that is being built.* **Liam** *is giving instructions to the workers, men and women.*

Standing by, not hired, a group of people including **John**, **Brian**, **Dan** *and* **Dan***'s* **Wife**. *This group in a block, motionless, silent, staring.*

Liam (*to a worker*)   Level that patch, step nimble, don't be leaving it all to the roller . . . (*To another.*) Break them smaller or you'll get no day's task marked up for you. (*To another.*) Root out them bushes . . .

JP *who is engineer of the works enters. He is followed by* **Mickeleen**. *There is something strange in* **Mickeleen***'s attitude. In fact he is considering warning* **JP** *that* **Malachy** *is coming to shoot* **JP**.

Sir, this stretch will be ready for the roller next –

JP (*turns to* **Mickeleen**)   My good man, what are you following me for?

Liam   Clear off, O'Leary!

Mickeleen *exits.*

JP (*turns to* **Liam**)   Yes?

Liam   This stretch will be ready for the roller on Thursday.

JP *sighs over the sorry plight of the workers and the futility of the works.* **Liam** *misinterprets* **JP**'*s attitude*

It's not my fault if they're not doing the work. And some of them are complaining that the stones are field stones, not quarry stones. They're not able to work, sir.

JP *sighs again looking at the group standing by.*

Liam   I've told them, but they won't go away for me.

Mickeleen *has entered again, this time from another direction, and is watching* **JP**.

JP (*sees* **Mickeleen**)   What does that man want? What is he following me for? (*Calls to* **Mickeleen**.) What do you want, man? There's nothing here for you. I can't employ you if you haven't got a work permit. (*Continues to* **John**'*s group.*) I cannot employ you. Listen, I believe the government will reconsider its policy, I am very hopeful and maybe – soon – food will be distributed. (*No reacton from group.*) . . . Listen, the Quakers have set up a soup kitchen in Shaftstown: they require you to say or do nothing: it's a long way, I know, but you will get soup there. (*No reaction.*) . . . Have you permits? Then be off, be off with you! If this interference continues I shall have to call the soldiers. I'll have to call the soldiers, I will, and all work will be suspended. (*To* **John**.) I haven't the power to employ you, man.

John   Did I ask?

JP *and* **Liam** *move away.* **Mickeleen** *nervously looking after them and looking off.*

Mickeleen   Hah, Seán? Why should I protect anyone? And I don't know what thing it is you're waiting for. Hah, Seán?

Dan   Talk for us, Michael.

Mickeleen   Mickeleen Cam, Micheleen Cam! Twisted and humpy, mind and body, a codger the cripple, talk for the big men? Ask King Johnny. Your brand of right is only keeping yourself standing straight, Seán? Your defiance will splinter if you move, Seán, will it?

JP *and* **Liam** *are returning.*

Liam   O'Leary!

Mickeleen   Why should I protect anyone? It's plain as day there's no one giving. Hah, Seán? The work is it ye want? Then take it! Take it! Let it be a practice for ye at taking!

JP ⎫ Please, please, my good man –
Liam ⎭ O'Leary! Mickeleen -

Mickeleen (*to* **JP**). Run, run, vastard, run for your life!

Liam *looks off, sees* **Malachy** *approaching, then races away.* **Mickeleen** *shouts 'Run' again to* **JP** *and goes forward, arms outstretched to stop* **Malachy** *who is entering.* **Malachy** *is carrying a gun, he has his face blackened and he wears a woman's dress over his clothes. He sweeps* **Mickeleen** *aside, levels his gun and shoots* **JP**. **JP** *falls to his hands and knees.* **Mickeleen** *watches* **Malachy** *running away. He knows he will not see* **Malachy** *again.*

JP *crawls on hands and knees to* **Mickeleen***'s feet.*

JP   Help me . . . Help me.

Mickeleen, *laughing and crying, starts to kick* **JP**.

Mickeleen   But why should we starve like dying plants! Hah, Seán? Humpy slaves can be tyrants too! Hah, Seán? (*Crying, continues kicking* **JP**.) Hah, Seán? Hah, Seán? . . .

Excepting **John**, *the group close in on* **JP** *kicking him, falling on top of him and on top of each other, taking his boots and the contents of his pockets.* **Mickeleen** *comes free of them and is crying, looking off in the direction* **Malachy** *has taken.*

Scene Ten

The King and the Queen

That night.

Mother, **Maeve** *and* **Donaill**, *and their belongings, on the roadside beside the ruin of their house.*

Off, approaching, **John**, *drunk, muttering to himself and shouting defiantly.*

John (*off*)   Hale and hearty still! . . . Still standing straight! . . . They won't get the better of me! . . . (*Entering.*) I'm Connor of Glanconor! (*The sight of the ruined house stops him only for a moment.*) . . . It won't best us, a chuid!

Mother *does not lift her head.*

Maeve (*harshly*)   Where were you?

John   'Hat, girl?

Maeve   I was searching, I couldn't find you – A gang of them, they came.

John   'Asy!

Maeve   Every house, and Danny's – Father Horan trying to stop them.

John   They won't best *me*!

Maeve   They said the rent, the rent, arrears, the rent.
The bailley – We couldn't stop them – I couldn't find you
– We're to move.

John   And the whiskey hut Clancy set up is tumbled too!

Maeve   Didn't you know this would happen?

John   What are you saying?

Maeve   But you done nothing!

John   'Hat? (*Surprised and offended by her remark.*) . . . Root
out them doors! Root out them doors and we'll make a
shelter. Go on. (*She does not obey. He addresses* **Mother**.) Is
Donaill asleep? . . . 'Tis a relief to him. Wurra, mo chailín,
hut-tut, not another word now. Look! I brought ye
something. (*He produces a bottle of whiskey.*) Whish – whish –
whish anois now, not another word from you, Sheeny, but
drink down a blogam and you'll see the good of it. And
we'll give a taste to the putackeen when he wakes. Go on,
Sheeny. (**Mother** *and* **Maeve** *drink a little.*) They killed the
engineer, then tumbled the whiskey hut. But I done
nothing wrong. Nor won't. I got that bottle off Danny.
They won't get the better of me! (*To* **Maeve**.) Not too
much now, mo pheata, or 'twill hurt you. (*He sets about
building a shelter.*) I'll throw up these doors and won't we be
secure against anything that's sent. And in a day or two
I'll find better place where they can't shift us so easy. Sure,
the Springtime is on us and look at all the holdings that'll
be going. We'll be better off than ever. Cause we'll last it.
(*He is finding it difficult to lift the door to make a roof for the shelter
he has built; he chuckles to himself.*) Oh, bo-bo-bo-bo-bo!
Maeve, come here and help me. (*She doesn't. He lifts the door,
completing the shelter.*) . . . If we had a dog now, like the
rambling man, we'd have place to keep our feet warm. But
sure any dog left in it would only eat the toes of a one.
Hah? What am I saying? In with ye there now. Sure,
there's lots can be done. (**Maeve** *retches. He moves towards
her.*) Oh bo, mo pheata!

Maeve (*harsh*)   Leave me alone!

Mother (*harsh*)   Leave her be!

Maeve *exits.* **Mother** *carries* **Donaill** *into the shelter.* **John** *carries in their possessions.*

John   And the meal is to be given out.

Mother *pauses in what she is doing until he adds.*

Yis, Sinéad: The Policy: they're going changing their minds.

They lie down in the shelter.

Silence.

Mother   Don't go asleep.

John   Hah?

Mother   . . . Did you say your prayers?

John   . . . Ary, phy – why – why wouldn't I. I said them coming home. I – Don't – Whisht.

Silence.

Mother   Don't go asleep.

John   Wurra, Sheeny –

Mother   All of Glanconor. Father Horan trying to stop them. And the same man is gone strange from all that's dying without the oil . . . Johnny?

John   Wurra, Sheeny, we'll be on top of the wheel yet. We'll be right with the Springtime. Draw in closer. We'll be – Hah? Weren't the Connors kings here once. Hah? And still. And still. And always married queens. Didn't we? There was enough of a hoult in you one time. And there will again, big and round, like any queen. You'll see. Uroo, mo vourneen –

Mother   No, no, stop, stop.

John   And the giggling of you, the Lord save us, nights. Draw in closer. Pull in Sinéad. Sheeny, mo chuid. The

childeen is asleep. Hah? And sure, she's off walking out
there. And, sure, you don't want to freeze.

Mother (*sits up, pulls away from him*)   We should have
went! They're there now, eating their nough, Marcus and
the rest. The only wonder is we're still alive . . . They say
it isn't too hard to get to England . . . Do you hear?
England isn't so far away.

John   Far or near.

Mother   But what's to become of us? No roof, no plan.
How can we escape, and the fever on top of it now?
There's hundreds making safe voyages . . . Johnny? And I
don't know what I do be thinking, walking over the dead
scattered about. I can't pray. And I want to tell you about
Brian's turf.

John   Whist. Sleep.

Mother   His turf. I stole it –

John   Don't.

Mother   I as good as killed him. I stole his turf for flour.

John   I'm not listening to you.

Mother   God knows I'm not fit to die yet!

John   Whisht – 'Asy – You don't understand.

Mother   But what's the use in –

John   I don't know!

Mother   We'll all die here.

John   Then let us!

Mother   Shhh! You're only being stubborn.

John   Stop.

Mother   The childre –

John   Don't.

Mother   The –

John   I'll look after them! I'll – Don't keep on.

Mother   Just, it's a quare thing if you'll allow –

John   Jesus – Stop – Christ – Woman! Isn't there enough trying to best me besides you! It won't get me. I don't understand it myself, but I have to live. Someone has to live. So don't keep on. Or that other strap rambling out there. Saying I'm doing nothing. Cause – I – will – live! I'm doing what I'm doing. How else can I? That holding is mine. That holding – *All* that land was Connors' once! And I'll not go. Not for landlord, devil, or the Almighty himself! I was born here, and I'll die here, and I'll rot here! . . . Cause there's food to be . . . The road-making is to . . . Cause there's . . . Cause I'm right.

Scene Eleven

The Queen Dies

A few evenings later. **John**, *seated motionless, in the ruin of his house.* **Maeve** *is somewhere about, looking off occasionally for the return of* **Mother**. **Donaill**, *asleep, in the shelter. In a second make-shift shelter on the opposite side of the stage is* **Dan**, *sitting up in a bed of straw, laughing and rambling away to himself. His* **Wife**, *Cáit, is dead beside him.*

A fire favours **Dan**'s *side of the stage. At the end of the scene,* **John**'s *side of the stage is in darkness,* **Dan**'s *is dimly lit by the fire.*

Dan   What year was I born in? 1782 they tell me, boys. There's changes since, Brian? There is, a mac. And Henry Grattan and Henry The Other and prosperity for every damned one. Hah? Yis – Whatever that is. (*Laughs.*) Oh, I'm alright, and herself is worse. Máirtín Hynes in Annagh Cross will forge me a pike in the morning. For the rebellion, Máirtín. There's a rising . . . Whisht! Who's in it? . . . Can't I hear ye breathing? . . . Oh, be off – be off –

be off. I've things to be doing. We have things to be doing,
Cáit . . . Is she dead? With your tight black face. Lord
have mercy or divil mend her: (*Laughs.*) one of the two will
be on the lookout for you. If I'm old enough for a spade,
Máirtín, I'm old enough for a pike, Máirtín. Though I
never killed. But we had the sport, 1798 yis, out all hours
under the bushes. But she was sprightly. She could sing . . .
She could sing . . . Why do I keep talking, Johnny? And
how many said that to me? And why do I? (*Laughs.*)
Because! . . . Oh, what way was she ever, but cold. Cold,
boys. Her feet worse nor the dog's nose through years
prodding me into the grave. Rise up, you bony óinseach,
and kindle the fire! . . . I'm afraid of the sleep in case of
the rats, Daniel, said Mother. Isn't it comical? And the
comical small piaties in '17 and, oh, a Thighearna, an t-
ocras mór, an droch shaoil! Your father was better man
with spade nor two cross Connors, four Dougans, or seven
Dineens. (*Laughs.*) And isn't he dead now, Mother? Yis.
Lallys' side of Clogher Bridge, near the water, 1822, and
little on him for the maggot after the rat had pleased
himself. But the C'ronor said he was drunk on poteen. I
suppose he was. But I liked him, in spite of all.

Maeve She's coming.

Dan Whisht! . . . But do you remember the wind, the big
wind blowing? 1839. What didn't it blow? (*Laughs.*) That's
how you lost your hair, Simon? What was I saying? Oh,
but do you remember the wedding – Oh, long before the
wind – the Union, Brian, in 1800? The marriage to start
off a brand new century and prosperity for every damned
one. And Rosaleen without a dowry. But isn't a good
woman better nor the finest dowry? And with a good man,
a dry bed, and pulling together . . . A strange little animal,
the rat.

Mother *enters, a piece of bread in her hand. She puts the bread in
front of* **John**. *She crawls into the shelter to look at* **Donaill**.

The fine suit they put on me one morning, with Murty
Dineen, and we laughing to be taken voting, like the forty

shilling farmers. We laughed. Well, we did. And took them off us again at noon and were each given a sixpence by a man by the name of Bully MacKiernan. Bhí go maith, is ní raibh go h-olc, till once at the fair of Turlough, Turley Connor – Yis, father to Johnny – split the Bully with a granite stone, and that put paid to the voting.

Maeve *has been watching* **Mother**. *Cautiously, she moves to where the bread had been left and takes it.* **John** *does not appear to notice, though she is directly in his line of vision.* **Maeve** *starts to wolf down the bread.*

Oh, the Connors were nobles and not to be bested; the Connors would do the brave thing always . . . Cáit? And weren't you alright a minute ago?

Mother *comes out of shelter; she sees* **Maeve** *eating the bread. She rushes at* **Maeve**. *They struggle. The remaining piece of bread falls.* **Maeve** *breaks away from* **Mother** *and runs into the shelter.* **Mother** *tries to salvage some of the crumbs but seeing the futility of it, she abandons it*

John *rises when* **Mother** *and* **Maeve** *are struggling. He does not want to see or hear what is going on before him.*

Dan *continues to speak, softly keening for his wife, during* **Mother**'s *speeches.*

Mother, **John** *and* **Dan** *form a kind of trio with* **Mother** *speaking lead*

Cold and silent is now your bed, damp is the blessed dew of night but the sun will bring warmth and heat in the morning and dry up the dew. But your heart will feel no heat from the sun. No. Nor no more the track of your feet in the dew. No. Nor no more the sound of your step in Glanconor where you were ever foremost among women. No. Cold and silent is now your bed.

My sunshine you were. I loved you better nor the sun itself. And when I see the sun go down I think of my girl and the black night of sorrow. For a storm came on. And my girl cannot return.

Life blood of my heart, she was brave, she was generous.
She was comely, she was clear-skinned. And when she
laughed – Did ye hear? And her hair – Did ye see? –
Golden like the corn. But why should I tell what everyone
knows? She is gone forever, she will return no more. Cold
and silent is her repose.

Mother   The bread, the bread, the bread for your father!
If he goes what's to happen to us? Connor! Move! Ketch
her and scald her! Oh, Lord in heaven, you strap! The
crumbs I went through hell to get! Take up the stick! –
Take up the stick! The fourteen miles again today: this
time off charitable people: their books I was prepared to
kiss, though they never asked me. Connor, will you move
now, or are you still engaged, defying all, standing in the
rubble of what you lost? What bravery! But he's doing
what's right he says. Right? Our noble men can afford
what's right. Will I keep stealing from the dying?

John   ⎫ (*turning away from her; an undertone*)   Don't keep
            ⎬ on.
Mother ⎭ You'll listen! Come forward to view your
            handsome childre. The cruit on one, the twist to
            her every part, her eyes without notion of a
            tear. And the belly black and swole on your
            heir. Did ever the vicious Connors of yore foster
            their likes? The leaders and chieftains!

A little movement from **John**, *leaning forward, to move off.*

You forgot us! – You forgot us! . . . He wouldn't go, no.
For why? Yis, we know – we've understood! – but how,
Lord, did he think us to live here? No rights or wrongs or
ráiméis talks, but bread, bread, bread. From where, but
myself – Not him, not You – but always the slave, the slave
of the slave, day after day, to keep us alive for another
famine.

A little movement from **John**, *stooping, to pick up a stick. He
hesitates.*

Take it up, yis, take up the stick!

John } *(a strong undertone)*   Don't keep on.
Mother } Jesus Christ above, what's wrong at all, and all
the clever persons in the world? Biteens of
bread are needed only. Life blood of my heart:
hunger, childre, pain and disease! – What are
we going through it for? Take us then! Take
her – Take him! It's nothing new to You to
take them, and roast them in hell if that's what
You want them for. For there must be other
ideas in Your mind. Well, they're there for You
now, for You, Policy or the Blight.

John *takes up the stick.* **Mother** *fears he will not use it. She
pauses, holding her breath.*

Dan's *voice rising for a moment, 'And when she laughed – Did ye
hear? And her hair – Did ye see? – golden like the corn . . .' Etc., to
end of keen. '. . . cold and silent is her repose'.*

Mother *(quieter more intense)*   Johnny. Are they to have my
life so easy? Would that be right? . . . Johnny, I've
understood your defiance, the hope you picked out of
nowhere. I've understood all along but it's not of my kind,
nor can it ever be. Now they have me prone, and I can
only attack your strength. But you will protect yourself.
They gave me nothing but dependence: I've shed that lie.
And in this moment of freedom you will look after my
right and your children's right, *as you promised*, lest they
choose the time and have the victory. *(She goes into the shelter
and lies down.)*

Mother, **Maeve** *and* **Donaill** *are now in the shelter which is
almost completely in darkness.*

John *moves to the shelter. We hear the stick rising and falling.
After a moment* **Maeve** *rushes out of the shelter and off. The sound
of the stick, rising and falling, continues for a few moments.*

Dan *resumes his rambling talk.*

Dan   Whisht now a minute and riddle me this. Bhí fear is
fear is fear . . . Sure I seen O'Connell once! Yis, yis, yis,

The Liberator – didn't we, Brian? We did. And we waved,
and he waved. And he smiled. On top of his horse. The
lovely curly head on him. He did, did, waved with his hat.
Aaaa, but the day we got our freedom! Emancy-mancy –
what's that, Nancy? – Freedom, boys! Twenty-nine was
the year and it didn't take us long putting up the new
church. The bonfires lit, and cheering with his reverence.
Father Daly, yis. And I gave Delia Hogan the beck behind
his back. I had the drop in and the urge on me. (*Laughs.*)
Oh! – Oh! – Oh! – Oh! that's alright, said Delia, winking,
but the grass is wet . . .

John *comes out of darkness and walks off. He has killed his wife
and his son.*

Whisht . . . A strange little animal. The auld is to be
deserted, Daniel, said Mother. Yis, I said, and married
herself that the Colonel had spoiled. Oh, we were both
past 'Collopy's Corner' and I had doubts I'd knock any
rights out of her. And didn't. And didn't. No one to tend
me now? As Jesus was noble and denied, he has long since
been repaying the closed doors to him in Bethlehem! He
has. And all the doors that's closed and black throughout
today will have to be repayed . . . Cáit! Cáiteen! Well,
you're a divil like myself. (*He laughs.*) Well you are! A
dancer, a topper! Well, isn't she? And she'll be first asked
at wake or wedding to sing. Oh, I married the blackbird,
boys, I did, I did. I married the blackbird, boys. I did. I
did. . . .

Scene Twelve

The Springtime

Before and as the lights come up:

John   Sheeny, Maeve, Donaill! The meal, it's come!
Marcus, Liam, Brian, Danny! It's come! Cáit, Malachy,
Mickeleen! It's come! . . .

It is Spring, 1847. **John** *is on a rise (or at some remove from* **Maeve** *and* **Liam** *whom we see later); a strange isolated figure; perhaps he has lost his senses: who can say? He walks off.* **Maeve** *is looking down at a corpse,* **Mickeleen**. **Liam** *enters, a piece of bread in his hand.*

Liam   The meal, it's come. (*He offers the piece of bread to her.*)

Maeve   No. O'Leary is the only name I'd accept anything from.

Liam   Some say Malachy is dead too: I don't know. Some say he's in America, a gang to him. Whichever, this country will never see him again.

Maeve   It'll see his likes.

Liam *offers the bread to her again.*

No. There's nothing of goodness or kindness in this world for anyone, but we'll be equal to it yet.

Liam   Well, maybe it'll get better.

Maeve   No.

Liam   And when it does we'll be equal to that too.

He puts the bread into her hand. She starts to cry.

Printed in the USA
CPSIA information can be obtained
at www.ICGtesting.com
LVHW041101171024
794057LV00001B/191